INBOX ZERO

INBOX
ZERO

How to Stop *Checking* Email
and Start *Finishing* It

IAN CHARNAS

ISBNs: 978-1-7325352-0-6 (paperback); 978-1-7325352-1-3 (ePub); 978-1-7325352-2-0 (Kindle)

Cover image of Inbox Zero badge used with permission from John Young of Nerd Merit Badges.

Graphic of email checking patterns adapted with permission from Jack Reeves.

Edited by Akiko Yamagata
Proofread by George Goga
Book design by Mayfly Design
Photography by Paul Sobota and Daniel Milner

Published by Inbox Zero Solutions, LLC
First printed 2018

My dear reader,

This book is dedicated to you, my fellow captive of a half-century-old messaging system run amok.

This way out!

Contents

Preface

My personal email story begins in the 1990s. Only a few friends and colleagues knew my email address, and whenever I received a new email, I got so excited! It was like getting a handwritten letter. I couldn't wait to read it. At that point, I was receiving one or two emails a day. When I started studying engineering at Case Western Reserve University, that number steadily grew to ten per day...then twenty. As I entered the professional world, my email volume grew to fifty emails per day, and then one hundred.

My first reaction to the growing volume of emails was just to work harder. I began spending most of my waking hours dealing with them, which caused me no small amount of anxiety and stress. When my inbox grew to 200 emails a day, I finally reached a breaking point. I knew I had to work smarter, not harder. I explored email productivity strategies for years before eventually developing the three-step solution I present in this book—and it has made a tremendous difference in my life. I went from spending six hours a day on email to just one sixty-minute session. In my current role managing an innovation center at an R1 research university, I send and receive an average of 210 emails per work day, and during my sixty-minute daily email session, I process every single one of them. I use the term *process*, and it's a crucial component of my approach to managing email. In the following pages, I'll define what it means to process emails so that you will have the tools to try it for yourself and see if it makes a difference in your life, too.

My framework is based on two decades of research on how to unburden yourself from email overload. Together, our goal will be to get to inbox zero, a concept popularized by productivity experts David Allen and Merlin Mann. If you've never experienced an empty inbox, you're in for a treat! If you're an inbox zero person already but you've struggled to keep it at zero, this might be the solution you've been looking for. In this book, you'll learn how to get to an empty inbox and, more importantly, how to spend less time getting email done so that you can free yourself to accomplish more important goals.

Introduction

Reading is the supreme lifehack. Distilled knowledge that often took years to assemble can be consumed in just a few hours. And the more you know about social psychology and human behavior, the better. Reading good psychology books lets you jump-start your education by absorbing what researchers, professors, and authors spent years putting together. I can't think of a single better way to empower yourself than that.

—Gregory Ciotti, author of *SparringMind* blog

The humble system we call email was devised in the 1960s as a way for early computer geeks to exchange simple text-only messages. Despite the technical limitations of a system designed more than fifty years ago, email has become our everything box. We attempt to store all of our information in our inboxes. We have repurposed the email inbox as a to-do list, instant messaging app, project management system, help desk ticketing platform, and document management solution. Each day, our inboxes are filled with order confirmations, calendar invitations, newsletters, social media notifications, and spam. The problem is that email is not designed to be our everything box. It does a great job at the one thing it was designed for—sending and receiving brief messages that are not time sensitive. Trying to use email for other purposes overloads our inboxes. Eventually, we start feeling overloaded ourselves.

One research study found that 85 percent of us report feeling email overload. Of course, email *can be* a productive way to communicate. It helps us feel up to date, it creates a record of conversations, and it provides a simple means of archiving and retrieving information. But have you ever returned to your computer after a string of meetings feeling nervous about how many new emails may be waiting for you? Do you find yourself staying late or checking emails on nights and weekends? Have you felt the irresistible pull to look at your smartphone when an email notification made it buzz? Do you worry about things falling between the cracks, or even worse, missing something really crucial? You are not alone. There are so many modern professionals who have reported feelings of information overload that it has attracted the attention of scientists around the globe.

An entirely new field of research has emerged to study how email and other technologies are affecting us. Few researchers in this new field have been as prolific as Gloria Mark, professor at the University of California, Irvine. She has published and presented over 150 papers in top journals and conferences and is a visiting senior researcher at Microsoft Research. Mark is one of those rare and adventuresome researchers whose work goes beyond surveys and laboratory experiments. She ventures into the real world to study professionals where they work in large corporations. Think of her as the Jane Goodall of email research, studying professional primates in their native habitats. In one study measuring email-induced stress, she strapped biometric sensors on participants to record heart-rate variability, fluctuations in heart rate that are a tell-tale indicator of stress. And what did she discover? Email is stressful! You could have guessed that one, right? No shocker there.

What was surprising, however, was the specific relationship between email and stress. With so much of our work being conducted over email, one might reasonably guess that the more time people spend on emails, the more work they would get done and the less stress they would feel. After all, it feels good to get work done, right? Strangely, she found the opposite. The more time people spend on email, the more stress they feel.

Mark's study rigorously confirmed what dozens of large-scale surveys had also suggested, that there is something unique about the way email stresses us out. Voicemail doesn't affect us in the same way. You won't find people frantically checking their voicemail seventy-seven times a day, as her study found professionals doing with email. Likewise, meetings and phone calls aren't considered as stressful as emails. Professionals may complain about the number of meetings on their calendars, but a Stanford University study showed that even though meetings or phone calls are just as likely to cause us to stay late at work, we tend to see email—and the amount of time we spend in email, specifically—as the main cause of stress in workplace communications.

How, then, can we use this information to our advantage? We know that the more time we spend on email, the more stress we feel. This leads us to ask whether the reverse is also true. If we could spend less time on email, could we reduce the anxiety we feel when we think about our inboxes? In fact, researchers have beat us to this question— and the answer, according to multiple studies from across the globe, is yes. Perhaps the largest of these was a multiweek study of 124 participants at the University of British Columbia, appropriately titled "Checking Email Less Frequently Reduces Stress." For one week, researchers Kostadin Kushlev and Elizabeth Dunn told half of their participants to limit their email checking to three times per day, while the other participants were told to check email as often as they wanted. The next week, they flipped their instructions. The email maximizers became the email minimizers and vice versa. Participants responded daily to a set of questions that measured their levels of stress.

The results were overwhelming. Participants checking email less frequently spent 20 percent less time in email and experienced a significant reduction in stress. How much less? About as much as people experience from relaxation techniques like meditating on peaceful imagery. Would you like your life with email to feel the same as picturing yourself floating in warm tropical waters? Step by step, this book will illuminate a roadmap to get you there. But first, we need to take a brief detour to understand how we got where we are today.

The Surprising History of Information Overload

Trying to answer every email as it comes in is like trying to drink from a fire hose. It's easy to be bowled over by the endless volume of emails arriving on a daily basis. However, we're not the first humans to feel overwhelmed. Ours is part of a long history of people searching for solutions to information overload.

The term *information overload* actually predates the modern internet. It was popularized in 1970 in the book *Future Shock*, a few years before the first electronic mail was sent across ARPANET, the precursor to the internet. That first message launched us on a path to information overload on an unprecedented scale, but the idea goes back much further than that. The seventeenth-century French scholar Adrien Baillet warned his contemporaries, worrying that scholars could soon be overwhelmed by the sheer volume of books being produced:

> We have reason to fear that the multitude of books which grows every day in a prodigious fashion will make the following centuries fall into a state as barbarous as that of the centuries that followed the fall of the Roman Empire. Unless we try to prevent this danger by separating those books which we must throw out or leave in oblivion from those which one should save.

Baillet sounded an alarm that we can appreciate in the internet age. He was alive during a transition in the volume of information being produced and feared that a technology invented two and a half centuries earlier had begun to represent a dire threat to civilization. The evil invention? A time-sucking device invented by Johannes Gutenberg called the printing press. Fortunately for Baillet and the rest of us, that device ultimately did not cause widespread barbarism. But it did birth an "infinite scroll" of books to which there was no end. The world was forever changed. Was this, then, the beginning of information overload? As it turns out, we're not yet even in the right millennium.

As we peel back further centuries, the theme of information overload can be found nearly everywhere. When the Roman philosopher

Seneca, born in the year 4 BCE, composed his plays on morality, he noted: "A multitude of books only gets in one's way." Even at the dawn of the common era, he found a good portion of written communication to be of middling value.

The book of Ecclesiastes, written as early as 450 BCE, complains: "Of making many books there is no end, and much study wearies the body." In the same way that we feel stressed by the endless stream of emails appearing in our inbox—seemingly too many for one person to handle—scholars living thousands of years ago expressed frustration at their inability to read all the books that had been written.

I can almost imagine this fictional scene 4,500 years ago: Gilgamesh in Mesopotamia, looking at the number of clay tablets that were being written and just throwing up his hands. "People! You've got to stop cc-ing me on all these clay tablets! I have seventeen unread tablets this month alone—I just can't."

If there is a lesson here, it's that information overload is nothing new—and the good news is that we can overcome it, just like the scholars of antiquity. How did they get out from under the crushing weight of the "multitude of books?" They invented new ways to deal with it. They created indexes and encyclopedias that made it faster to find the information they were looking for. They invented cutting and pasting (and I mean physically, as a means of assembling manuscripts). They adapted.

We are not alone in our quest. Just as those early scholars used new tools for managing book overload, we must devise a new strategy to manage email overload.

You Are Losing Valuable Time to Email

How much time do we actually spend on email? It depends on whom you ask, but my favorite answer is "Too much!" According to a large study that Adobe conducted of more than 1,000 white-collar professionals, the average US office worker spends 5.2 hours a day on email.

Where do we find those 5.2 hours? Adobe's study and others have found that we fill every moment of our schedules with email. We're doing emails at night and on weekends, during our vacations, before getting out of bed in the morning, and even while we're in the restroom. Some of us even do emails at funerals.

By any behavioral measure of addiction, we are unquestionably addicted to email. In a healthy brain engaged in nonaddictive behaviors, the pursuit of a reward followed by its attainment leads to the feeling of being satiated—of having had enough. For email, there is no "enough." We keep checking it, even when we should really be doing something else.

When we're working under a deadline, for example, we'll forgo eating, forget to drink water, and even endure pain rather than step away from our desks to use the restroom. Yet somehow, in the midst of this, we still find time for email. Despite our best attempts to focus on important work, the endless buffet of distraction offered by Gmail and Outlook continues to lure us in.

Even though email may be necessary for most of us in the modern world, we'd like to have more control of it. Putting you in control of your email is the goal of the book, and to accomplish this, we will draw on psychological strategies that are more powerful than the compulsion to incessantly check your email.

A Three-Step Science-Based Strategy

This book presents a three-step strategy that took me from spending six hours a day on email down to spending less than sixty minutes, and significantly reduced my stress along the way. Since I began using this system, I no longer worry about what might be waiting for me in my inbox, and I no longer fear missing something crucial. This system works because it employs a treasure trove of lessons derived from behavioral psychology. In this book, we will explore the hidden forces behind email overload and learn how to overcome it using a set of powerful psychological tools. If you've ever been on Facebook and suddenly realized that hours went by without your having noticed, then you know how powerful these invisible forces can be. Our strategy will be to turn the tables and use the science of psychology to our own advantage. As we progress toward our goals, distilled knowledge from countless research studies representing the life pursuits of hundreds of scientists will come to our aid in surprising ways.

My hope is that you will use this system to reclaim precious time in your life and set better boundaries and expectations when it comes to communicating with other professionals in the digital world.

So, without further delay, here's a preview of our three-step science-based strategy:

Step 1 – Pause your inbox. What if I told you there was a secret pause button in your inbox, and if you pressed it, no new emails could come in? We're going to go over what that means and why you would want to do that. It involves a new app called Boomerang, which is going to help cure your email overload.

Step 2 – Process every email and get to inbox zero. This doesn't mean you'll necessarily reply to each email right away, but I'll give you a strategy for dealing with emails efficiently. Your goal is to get them all out of your inbox, even the ones that are really difficult. As an important part of this step, I'll provide instructions on how to set up a proper organizer to manage your tasks, so you can stop using your email inbox as a to-do list.

Step 3 – So now your inbox is empty, and it will stay that way until you choose to unpause it. There are no emails to distract you. What do you do now? Leave it paused and move forward on ambitious projects that will define your career.

Once you have mastered the basics, explore the Expert Mode chapter at the back of the book, which contains advanced tips for productivity.

Pause Your Inbox

R esearchers believe the reason email causes so much stress is that it interrupts us over and over again throughout our workday, ruining our focus and preventing us from getting things done. Every time a pop-up notification dings or we impulsively check our inbox, we lose focus on what we are doing. These frequent interruptions cause stress. When we experience stress, our breathing shortens and our heartbeat dramatically changes. Instead of the carefree and highly variable heartbeat pattern seen during low-stress conditions, our hearts beat out a hypercontrolled rhythm reminiscent of the loud, steady heartbeat heard in scary movies. During this elevated state of anxiety and mental strain, some people experience tension headaches and migraines. This stress also causes cortisol levels to rise in our blood, which can interfere with learning and memory, elevate our blood pressure, and even block the action of our immune system. Stress is bad for us, and even without research studies to confirm this, we've felt firsthand what stress does to us physically, mentally, and emotionally.

We're going to install a pause button in your inbox to put you back in control. Those dings will be gone forever; there will be no reason to impulsively check your inbox, and nothing will appear in your inbox until you're ready for it.

Install Boomerang and Gain Control

The pause button is part of an app called Boomerang. This app works as a plugin for Gmail or Outlook on your desktop computer or laptop, and there's also a mobile Boomerang app for your smartphone or tablet.

Go ahead and install it. Visit boomerangapp.com and select the version that works for you. It takes less than a minute to do so, and if you end up not liking it, you can always remove it.

I'll wait while you do this.

Did you really do it? No? You won't get the maximum value from this book if you don't give this a try. You owe it to yourself to experience the feeling of being in control of your email. Besides the pause button, the app comes with several other powerful features, including the ability to schedule emails to be sent later. Boomerang also has the ability to have emails pop back into your inbox if you don't receive a reply, so you can make sure nothing escapes your iron-clad follow-through.

Once you've added Boomerang, click the Pause button. This is your shield. Nothing gets through until you're ready. Step 1 is now complete. While you revel in the satisfaction of already being one-third complete with your journey to inbox zero, let's look at why this is so powerful.

Receive Email on Your Own Time

Imagine an arcade game where each email is an enemy spaceship ready to attack your time and focus. You never know when a new email is going to appear, so you have to check all the time! Imagine, though, if you could turn on a freeze ray and stop those emails in place. If you can be absolutely sure that no new emails will appear in your inbox, the tension you feel to always be checking will disappear.

Scientists have a name for this technique: precommitment. If you wanted to lose weight, you might go through your kitchen cabinets and throw out all the cookies and chips while you still have the will-power so they don't tempt you later when you no longer have the ability to resist. If you wanted to exercise more, you might put on your exercise clothes as soon as you wake up and just see what happens. If you're Odysseus, you might ask your crew to tie you to the mast so you won't be lured to a watery demise by a Siren's song. In each case, you're setting yourself up to make good behaviors easier and bad behaviors harder. Pausing your inbox makes it difficult to be distracted by email and easier to focus on things that really matter.

Your emails are important, but they're hardly the most import-ant work you do. Yes, responding to an email five seconds after it came in might make you feel powerful in a "Look what I can do" kind of way, but that dashed-off message offers limited value. If you can finish a task in under a minute, it probably doesn't reflect the deep-est value you can create. It might make you feel busy, but we must never confuse busyness with productivity. Your career will be made on your ability to accomplish large, complex projects—not your abil-ity to answer emails immediately.

You might be thinking, *I can't do this. I'm going to miss something crucial.* Don't worry. We're going to change how you work and use email so that your colleagues don't rely on email for urgent requests to you. Later on, we'll communicate this change to your team and get them on board so they use appropriate communication channels (like the phone) for questions that are all-caps URGENT. I promise, you can do this. For the time being, though, give yourself permission to experiment. You're just trying this to see if it works.

Conserve Your Willpower

You may be wondering: why pause your inbox instead of just not looking at it? Because it would deplete your willpower.

The longer you resist a temptation, the harder it becomes to resist. If you want to avoid eating the remainder of a box of delicious Thin Mints cookies, you need to hide them from yourself, or, better yet, get someone else to hide them so you don't even know where they are.

Willpower is the ability to resist short-term temptations in order to meet long-term goals. Research shows that you get a fixed amount of willpower each day. Use it up, and that's when you lose the ability to delay gratification. That's when you cave in.

Email is a tempting short-term goal: it can feel good to get in there and take care of a couple of emails. We use this diversion to procrastinate on our long-term goals. I've been guilty of this. I'm responsible for putting together a monthly newsletter. It takes about three hours, and I blocked off time on my calendar to do this well before the deadline, to give my colleagues plenty of time to review it. Then, when the time came for me to work on it, what did I do? I thought, *Hmm, I should be doing that difficult three-hour project . . . but it's not really due for two weeks. I'll do some emails instead.* I found myself on the path of least resistance, mucking around in my email. The day before the newsletter was supposed to go out, I was suddenly in a frantic rush to get it done. I sent a desperate email to my colleagues: "URGENT: REVIEW BEFORE END OF DAY." Where did the urgency come from? It came from my lack of preparation, because finishing a dozen tiny tasks like responding to emails felt better than trying to start one large task. Does this sound familiar? We can do better!

When our inboxes are paused and emptied—which we'll get to in the next step—there's no temptation to look at them. You will be absolutely certain that there are no emails for you to read and respond to. There are no easy little tasks you can use to distract yourself. The path of least resistance will take you to the challenging tasks that offer the greatest reward.

Pull the Plug on the Cognitive Slot Machine

We spend a lot of time on email and smartphones because they have addictive properties.

They are so addictive that some high schools have begun to lock up students' smartphones for the duration of the school day in order to put a lid on the distractions they cause. In one Boston-area high school, students' cell phones are locked in thick gray security pouches. The students' addiction is so deep, however, that even when they can't see the screen or touch the buttons, they keep the pouches on their desk and even clutch them for comfort. While some students may complain about their "toy" (their words!) being taken away, teachers are reporting dramatic improvements in students' abilities to pay attention during class. The ability to "pause" those distractions has led to academic improvements across the board.

On average, we check our desktop email 74 times per day. That means that during a typical work day, email is interrupting us every 6.5 minutes, and that's just desktop email. If you then add in the 76 times a day we check our smartphones, we're now getting interrupted on average every 3 minutes and 18 seconds. It's incredibly disruptive, and amazingly, we are doing this to ourselves. Again and again, we are drawn to our email as if by a magnetic force. What is it about email that makes it this addictive?

Researchers think one of the reasons we get pulled in is the same thing that makes slot machines so popular: variable reward. We check and check our inboxes, and sometimes we get something we really want: an email response that we've been waiting for or notification of a large number of likes for our Facebook post. We don't know when these rewards will appear, so we check often. So email is like a cognitive slot machine. We can't help but spin again. This is why Instagram and Facebook use infinite scroll. You keep on scrolling and more and more images appear. It's like digital Pringles. We can't have just one.

We're going to pull the plug on the slot machine. Now that you've paused your inbox, you have removed email as a source of distraction, and are well on your way to defeating its addictive lure.

Eliminate Context Switching Costs

When your computer chimes with an email notification, it interrupts you and breaks your concentration. After you're done taking care of the email, it takes you a while to refocus. Do that a hundred times a day, and you've lost more time than you might want to admit. By pausing your inbox and taking care of your emails in one efficient batch, you avoid losing that time.

Switching Tasks Takes Time

The field of psychology sometimes uses the term *task switching* to refer to changes of focus, but I'm borrowing the more popular term *context switching* from computer science literature, referring to when a computer processor switches its attention from one program to another. During this time, the computer is merely copying data into working memory, so the program isn't able to start running yet. Think of those icons you see while a program is loading: the hour glass or the spinning beach ball. This wasted time is similar to the context switching cost—the penalty a computer pays for trying to rapidly switch from one running process to another.

Your brain is not exactly a computer, but the idea of context switching is a good analogy for what happens in your brain when you switch from one task to another. It slows you down. When you are deep in thought and your computer bings with an email notification, it takes a while for your brain to catch up: *Whoa, what's going on? Ok, we're doing something new? What exactly was this email conversation about? Do we remember where the discussion left off?* During this time, your conscious mind waits while the rest of your brain retrieves the details about this email chain from long-term memory. Later, after you finish that reply, you'll lose context switching time again as you attempt to refocus on your original task.

Researchers have measured the time lost to context switching from sixty-four seconds to as long as twenty-three minutes. Let's use the conservative figure and say it takes only sixty-four seconds. If you are checking your desktop email seventy-four times a day, that's over an hour and a half you are losing every day to context switching, to basically nothing. Over the course of a year, that's more than forty-six entire work days lost to context switching. Balderdash, you might say. It sounds impossible: we'd like to think we would notice an effect that large.

Science can be trusted only if its findings can be repeated by others—that's the fundamental principle behind its objectivity. What if we could demonstrate the cost of context switching to ourselves in real life, outside of the laboratory? Let's use a simulation game to do that, just as psychologists would do in the lab. In this exercise, you're going to write down a list of names.

Morgan	Jeremy	Cassie	Zena	Mitchell	Andrew

How quickly do you think you could write the first name here (Morgan)? Maybe three seconds? With six names, at three seconds each, it might take you eighteen seconds to write all of these, yes? Let's test this.

In the first blank row, use a pencil and write these names, one at a time, while timing yourself. You'll write M-O-R-G-A-N, then J-E-R-E-M-Y, and so on. Remember to time yourself.

Next, we're going to model context switching. In the second row, instead of writing one name at a time, you're going to write out the first letter of each name, then the second letter of each name, and so on. So in the first column you'll write M, in the second column you'll write J, all the way to the A in the last column. Then you'll return to the first column and fill in the second letter of each name, and so forth until you've written out each name completely. Again, remember to time yourself.

If you really try this, instead of just imagining it, you'll find that as you switch from one name to the next, it takes you a moment to think about the next letter before you can write it. This is the time lost to context switching. It took me thirteen seconds to write the names sequentially and forty-three seconds with context switching—more than three times as long.

Admittedly, this is a bit contrived. Can this exercise really represent what it's like to switch between tasks? When researchers test this, they use various games. The game might involve switching from a math question to a reading exercise. Or you might be asked to press different buttons depending on whether an even or odd number appears on the screen, and then switch back and forth from that to pressing different buttons based on whether a vowel or consonant is displayed. Psychologists have been at this for a half century, and they've consistently found that we lose time when we switch from one context or topic to another.

In the exercise above, you might also have noticed feeling annoyed when you were forced to context switch. This is the hidden cost of rapidly switching tasks: stress. You've experienced this feeling before. When you're in the middle of wordsmithing an important presentation and the phone rings, or when you're working on an urgent report and someone knocks on your door. Being snapped out of your mental flow like that can be very jarring. More and more in the digital age, uninterrupted time is becoming a luxury in the professional workplace. When we need to get real work done, we turn off our phones and isolate ourselves in coffeeshops or the conference room where we can work without interruptions.

Do One Thing and Do It Quickly

We are not the first to notice that you work faster if you focus on just one task and keep doing it until it's done. This is the idea behind the assembly line designed by Henry Ford's team. They found that workers are much more efficient if they don't have to switch back and forth between different tasks. Do just one thing, and do it quickly. That's how the well-choreographed ballet of baristas at Starbucks can get you a coffee in 20 seconds or a custom-blended drink in under 90 seconds.

This is also how you'll save time on email. When you do email, do only email. During the rest of your day, you'll use the pause button so you won't be interrupted by an unending stream of messages. You'll find that the benefits go beyond saving time—it's really about reducing stress, which, as you'll recall from the introduction, is proportional to the amount of time you spend in email.

Limit Your Interruptions

> Email is a wonderful thing for people whose role in life is to be on top of things. But not for me; my role is to be on the bottom of things. What I do takes long hours of studying and uninterruptible concentration.
>
> —Donald Knuth, legendary computer scientist,
> who liberated himself from email on January 1, 1990

Imagine that you're concentrating on an important project and an email pops up and interrupts you. Or maybe you have notifications disabled, but some part of your brain keeps nudging you, *Hey, check your email*. It's like someone physically poking you. Being poked can be startling—it doesn't feel good. But imagine that you are receiving these pokes 121 times every day, which is the number of emails received by the average office worker.

What if you had a choice in how these pokes were delivered? Option A, you get poked randomly throughout your day. You never know when the next one's coming, and they never end. There is no "time out" period when you are protected from being poked. This is what email is like today. Your brain is constantly on alert, watching out for these pokes. That's why your brain keeps reminding you, *Hey, check your email.* Your brain can never consider the task done.

This constant availability is the default in today's society, but it's not the only option. If you are conscientious about how your time is spent, there is an option B. Instead of those pokes coming randomly throughout your day, they can happen in one batch, concentrated in just one hour. The best part is you get to pick when that hour is. So for the rest of the day, you will be free from being poked. The part of your brain that was keeping a watchful eye on your email can now rejoin the rest of your brain in focusing on the task at hand.

When you pause your inbox and process your email batch to zero, all your pokes are done with and your brain knows it. It will stop reminding you to check your email.

Humans Can Focus on Only One Thing at a Time

We all think we're great at multitasking, but when that belief is tested through experiments, it turns out it's not really true. We're actually terrible at multitasking, with very few exceptions.

Studies show we can often rate other people accurately, but when it comes to rating ourselves, we have an inflated sense of our ability to multitask. That's why even people who themselves text and drive get angry when they see others doing the same thing. When it comes to our own behaviors on the road, we think, *Hey, it's no big deal. I'm really good at juggling two things at once.* Unfortunately, we're not. Even talking on a hands-free phone while driving increases our errors by over 100 percent! Of course, that doesn't apply to us, right?

This overestimation is called confidence bias. It's why 94 percent of college professors rate themselves as above average, and over 45% of drivers believe they rank among the most skillful 20%. Of course, neither of these is mathematically possible. Our brains are very good at deluding us, which is why we think that we can write emails while we're talking on the phone or listening at a meeting. Overconfidence bias allows us to believe that we are amazing at multitasking, at least until someone in a meeting asks us for our thoughts and our look of panic makes it plain to everyone in the room that we hadn't been following as closely as we would have liked to believe.

Multitasking is often considered a kind of mental juggling act. I was fortunate to interview world champion juggler Charles Peachock, to ask him how he maintains focus while performing. Peachock was featured on the hit show *America's Got Talent*, on which he made a record six appearances—taking him further than any juggler in the show's ten-year history. This success has made him the only juggler in history to be featured in *People* magazine. Peachock knows a thing or two about focus.

He describes focus in terms of background tasks and foreground tasks. Peachock has honed his eye-hand coordination over many years so that a simple act like juggling three objects doesn't require his focused attention—provided those objects are not on fire, which is a distinct possibility in his profession. The work that his eyes and muscles need to do to keep those objects in the air effectively fades into the background, leaving his mind free for foreground tasks, like having a conversation. However, if he has to juggle a set of sharp knives while balancing a sword on his forehead and, why not, another sword on top of that one just to make it hard—well, that is definitely a foreground task, and it's not very likely you'll be able to reach him on the phone at that particular moment in time.

Email is a foreground task: we need to recall long-stalled conversations, be thoughtful about how we decline a request, and remember to double-check our spelling and grammar. The problem is that we think it's a background task. We can breathe, drink water, or munch on our lunches while doing emails only because those are all background tasks. The parts of our brains doing those tasks have been trained by years of experience to the point where we can breathe and chew with nearly zero mental effort. However, it's a mistake to think we can focus our minds on preparing that major presentation while simultaneously responding to emails. As much as confidence bias makes us think we can handle both, tackling two foreground tasks at once is the office equivalent of juggling heavy bowling balls in a seven ball cascade: the science shows it's just not possible.

Batch Your Emails to Reduce Stress

Research on email overload has found that even when we receive a large number of emails every day, it's not the volume of emails we receive that causes us to feel overwhelmed. In fact, the person receiving ten emails a day and the person receiving a hundred a day might feel the same amount of email-related stress.

> Counterintuitively, though, the stress is <u>not</u> caused by the sheer volume of emails. It is caused by the chaotic way that we typically process them, and by the fact that new emails arrive while we are answering existing ones.
>
> —Alex Iskold, managing director of Techstars NYC start-up accelerator

If email volume doesn't lead to email overload, then what does? The answer is one that we might know intuitively based on how stressed we get knowing our next "poke" could come at any time. That's right, it's the chaotic way in which our emails arrive that wreaks havoc on our nerves. A study of 2,000 professionals in the United Kingdom showed that stress highly correlates with receiving push notifications and with leaving email open all day. Let's look at a visual representation that helps illustrate this effect.

The figure on the next page represents the work days of two imaginary people. The dark gray is the time they spend on email, and the light gray is the time they have available for focused work. The top graph shows someone who compulsively checks their email throughout the day, continually self-interrupting and disrupting their focus.

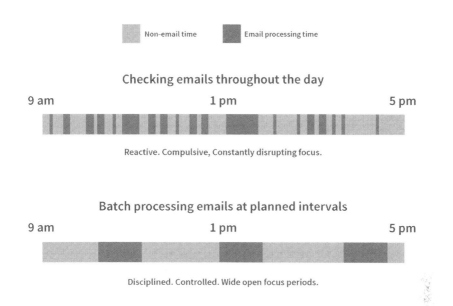

Non-email time   Email processing time

Checking emails throughout the day

9 am   1 pm   5 pm

Reactive. Compulsive, Constantly disrupting focus.

Batch processing emails at planned intervals

9 am   1 pm   5 pm

Disciplined. Controlled. Wide open focus periods.

The bottom graph shows someone who does email in batches, preserving large blocks of uninterrupted time to dive deeper into challenging work. Not only can the person in the bottom graph finish greater amounts of more difficult (and hence more valuable) work, the less frequent interruptions mean this person experiences significantly less email-related stress. Using the pause button to concentrate our email time during set intervals benefits not only our productivity but our mental and physical health as well.

STEP 2

Get to Zero

In the interviews I've conducted with professionals in various industries on their email habits, I found two basic email processing styles—checkers and finishers. Checkers are overwhelmed by their email and have chosen to "give up the fantasy that they could ever respond to all of their emails." With an ever-growing inbox, checkers read a few emails that seem most important, respond to a subset of those, and call it a day. When asked how they prevent things from falling through the cracks or how they ensure they respond to important messages, the most common answer was that they expect the sender to keep resending the message if it is truly important. The checkers I spoke with reported lower feelings of email-related stress, because they do not view email as a responsibility. If you've ever caught a glimpse of a friend's or colleague's inbox with 14,000 unread emails, you may know a checker. If a wave of anxiety washed over you at the sight of that, you are most likely an email finisher.

Finishers are the people you can rely on for a response. When finishers open their inbox, they see it as a list of items they need to deal with completely. If you did a personality assessment on these individuals, they would likely rate high in conscientiousness and they may list dependability as an important personal value. For finishers, email is a greater source of stress because they see it as an incoming stream of responsibilities. They will have devised some way of making sure things don't fall between the cracks—perhaps marking emails as unread, starring them, or keeping them open in a new window until they've sent a response. Finishers might archive emails that they've already handled to keep their inbox to less than one page. The challenge for them is that some emails seem perennially stuck. Try as they might, there are messages that have been in limbo for days or weeks or even years. Every time they see those messages, they think, *Oh, gosh—I really ought to respond to that one*. Does this sound like you or someone you know? The problem is that the longer you wait, the more embarrassed you feel that you haven't responded and the harder it becomes to actually respond.

Regardless of whether you have 10,000 unread emails or just 20 stubborn ones, you can apply the same approach to handling them and managing your inbox going forward. The core idea with inbox zero is to process all the messages in your inbox and then archive them. I handle 210 emails a day, and processing them takes me about sixty minutes using the techniques we're about to go over. My email is then done for the day. I don't look at it again. This may sound like a lot of emails, but I know others who receive many more. Alex Iskold, the managing director of the start-up incubator Techstar's New York City office, can get 400 emails in a single day, and he processes every one.

In this chapter, you'll learn how to process your email and achieve inbox zero. For each email that arrives, you'll learn a set of four actions you can take to get it out of your inbox. As you will see, this is not merely a list of tips and advice—it's a rigorous system you can apply to each and every email you receive. Think of it as a complete mental flowchart that helps you make fast decisions about what to do, no matter what appears in your inbox. With these tools, email finishers will actually be able to routinely get through all their emails, while email checkers can look forward to a newfound sense of control over the chaos of their inboxes.

Stop Using Your Inbox as Your To-Do List

Before we can explore a system that will get us to inbox zero, we need to make a fundamental change in how we think about email. We live in our inboxes because we use them as to-do lists that we never seem to finish. Despite popular belief, email is not meant to be a task management system. There's no way to order items based on priority, there's no sense of a due date, there are no milestones or dependencies, there's no simple way to onboard new team members so they can see the work in progress...I could keep going. Email was created to send messages and nothing more. When we try to use it to organize our work, we end up with screen after screen of tasks that are not getting done. The remedy is something the modern workplace seems to have forgotten: the organizer. Let's develop a framework we can use to build our own task organizer. This is a tool we'll need later as we implement the email processing techniques that will get you to inbox zero.

One of the most popular systems for organizing work is David Allen's Getting Things Done, or "GTD," as it's known to fans. His book, of the same name, has sold millions of copies, and its sales show no signs of slowing down. The book's core offering is a way of taking unfinished tasks and projects out of your mind and putting them into a system you can trust, so that your mind no longer needs to remind you of your task list and you can focus on things that are truly important to you. I use GTD every day: it's how I organize my work and my personal projects.

What follows is my personal task organization system, plus some added tips and tricks I've collected over the years. Of course, your mileage on this system might vary. One of my favorite science quotes is from Wernher von Braun, the German aerospace engineer and early rocket scientist, who came to the United States after World War II. He famously said, "One good test is worth a thousand expert opinions." As you read the following strategies and try them out, judge for yourself what works for you. I'll share just one piece of advice:

don't wait to find the "perfect" system. Dive right in, start trying things, and see what works. A good-enough system today is better than a perfect system months from now.

Create an Organizer

The first step to using an organizer is to decide on the format. How are you going to store your tasks? Some people use pieces of paper. If you go this route, GTD recommends using full-size loose-leaf paper and dedicating an entire sheet to each task (rather than adding many tasks to one piece of paper). However, I haven't met any GTD practitioners who still use paper: you can't access the piece of paper sitting on your desk if you're on the go. Instead, we use multiplatform apps that are instantly accessible from desktops, laptops, and mobile devices, no matter where our work takes us on a given day.

One of the most popular organizer apps, and the one I use, is a free one called Trello. It uses digital cards that let you gather your thoughts and notes along with checklists and file attachments for each task. This gives you a complete view of all details associated with a to-do item on a single screen. Let's go step by step through the process of setting up a task-management system in Trello, starting with an overview.

As I go through the unfiltered, unorganized messages in my email inbox, some of them will inevitably represent tasks that I need to do but that I don't have the time to do immediately. Instead of leaving those emails in my inbox to remind me to do the tasks, I transfer the associated tasks to Trello and then immediately archive those emails. In Trello, I create a card to represent each task and collect all of the details in one place. These cards are then organized into the following lists:

- Done – completed tasks
- Action Items – well-scripted, immediately actionable tasks
- Projects – long-term and multistep work

- Waiting For – items that are stuck or waiting on someone else
- Someday/Maybe – ideas for the future

Here is an image of how I set up my lists in Trello. Notice that I haven't added any cards yet; we'll get to that next. First, let's talk in detail about what goes in each list. If you'd like to follow along with me, you can sign up for a free account at trello.com.

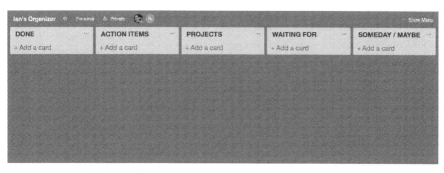

New organizer board with empty lists

Script Out Action Items

An important part of using this organizing system successfully is to distinguish a project from an action item. An example of a project is buying a house. Chances are, you can't sit down and immediately accomplish that. If that's on your to-do list, you will forever skip over it and look for something easier to do. But if you think about what's involved in getting that project done, you can generate an action item. For example, "Call realtor at 555-1212. Schedule an appointment to see 123 West Elm Street on Saturday at 3pm." Action items are scripted out so that you have access to everything you need to accomplish the task. By making the action items detailed and doable, you've removed some of the major obstacles impeding your progress. There are no more decisions to make, no more information to look up. It's very satisfying to see how much you can get done once you've separated action items from projects and turned amorphous to-dos into clear, well-scripted goals.

As you begin to add your to-dos to your organizer, decide first whether it's an action item (a task that you can complete in one brief work session) or if it's a project (longer-term work that will take multiple action items to complete). If it's an action item, script it out for yourself. Be thorough! Don't tell yourself, "Return humidifier," because you need the actions to be defined, not implied. Tell yourself this instead: "Call

ACTION ITEMS ...

Call (216) 555-7665. Ask vendor how you can return the humidifier from order #54321.

≡ ⏀ 1

+ Add another card

Our first Trello card

(216) 555-7665. Ask vendor how you can return the humidifier from order #54321." Here, you've given yourself all the information you'll need to get this done.

When you get around to making this phone call, the vendor should give you instructions for the return. Those details can go on the "back" of the card. Click on the card, and you'll see a window where you can add notes ("must be returned in original packaging") and attachments (such as the prepaid shipping label from the vendor). The image on the next page shows what the back of the card looks like after these changes. Once you've completed the task, you can move it to the Done list.

You might have noticed that I put the Done list first. It's because I like to see how many tasks I've accomplished. It motivates me to see this list grow. It also reminds me to focus on making progress on my action items and *not* on fiddling with my organizational system.

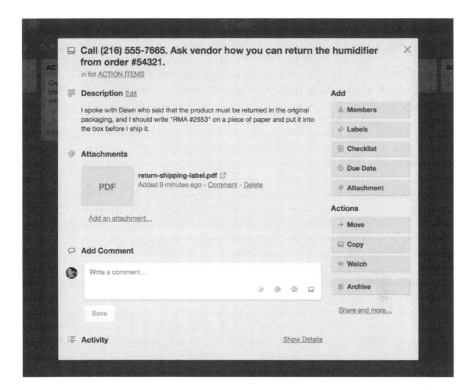

Additional details may be placed on the back of our Trello card

To continue marching forward, create an action item for the next actionable step. Now that you've called the vendor and have the instructions for returning the humidifier, you're ready to script out the next step: mailing it back to the vendor. You're going to create a new action item for that—but before you do, think for a moment. Are you *really* ready to mail it? Is there anything you need to do first?

Remember that each action item must be truly actionable. If there's something preventing you from taking immediate action, it's likely you're going to succumb to the human tendency to avoid obstacles. You'll probably skip over the item—*Oh, I can't mail it because I haven't printed out the shipping label*—and look for something truly actionable. Your approach, then, is to create an action item from the obstacle: just add an action item to print out the shipping label. It may seem like we're dumbing this down for ourselves, and we are!

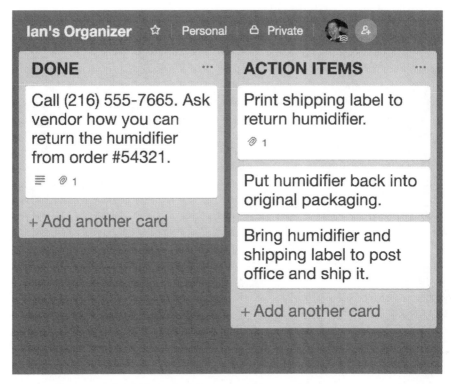

Add an Action Item for each step of the process

The easier these action items are, the more quickly we'll get them done. The pride you'll feel moving dozens of these cards to the Done list every day or week is worth it.

Separate Projects from Action Items

The purpose of the Projects list is to keep longer-term work from gumming up the works when you're tackling your Action Items list. On a regular basis, look at your list of projects and carefully script out the next actionable item. Let's say your supervisor emailed you, asking you to plan a staff retreat. Do not leave that in your email inbox! Add it to your list of Projects in your organizer, and decide on the next action item. Maybe your next step is to look through Yelp and generate a list of local entertainers, or to email last year's organizer to request a meeting. Or both!

Here's what our Trello organizer board looks like now:

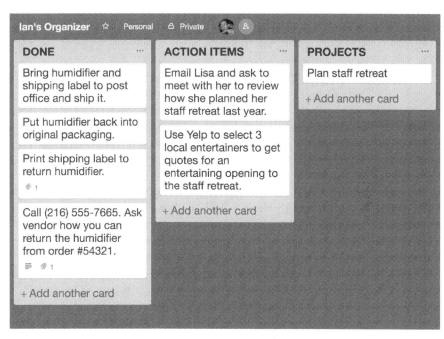

Create Action Items to represent the next actionable steps for your Projects

As you gather details and make decisions about the staff retreat, you can add this information to the back of the "Plan staff retreat" card so you have all your information in one place. You can use the attachments feature to store your graphic designer's printable invitation. You can use the sharing feature (which doesn't require a Trello account) to make it visible to your supervisor or coworkers. With the checklist feature, you can make a packing list, so that you'll remember all the necessary supplies on the day of the retreat.

Being able to script out truly actionable items is a crucial skill to develop, so before we move on, let's look at some additional examples. Consider whether "Prepare Q3 presentation" is really actionable or whether it's actually a project whose first action item is "Email Sam for last quarter's sales figures." Consider whether "Replace iPhone battery" enables immediate action or whether "Call Apple support at (800) 629-7753 to schedule iPhone battery replacement" is the next action you truly need to take. When a task is this concrete, you'll find you can do it even at the end of a stressful day when your mind is frazzled and your willpower is depleted.

Our Trello organizer has now expanded to this:

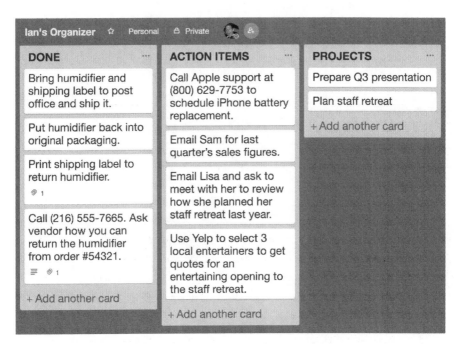

Continue to add Action Items and Projects to organize your work

When you put together your first organizer and begin to collect the reminders that are now scattered on sticky notes, in your calendars, in your head, and wherever else you store them, you may feel yourself getting excited. The thrill of being more organized comes from the release of tension from feeling overwhelmed by your to-do lists.

Don't Gum Up The Works

In my personal experience, the powerful step of scripting out a project's actionable items makes you more organized than a majority of professionals. To really keep that list actionable, you'll also need to consider what to do with tasks and projects that are not immediately actionable or are pending for any reason. You could be waiting on IT to upgrade your software before you can finish editing that video, but you want a place to store your storyboard, audio, and source footage. You could be waiting until June to send out the next monthly newsletter, but you want a place to collect your ideas so you don't forget them. Whatever the case, you don't need to let these things clog your Action Items or Projects lists. Move them instead to the Waiting For list. I find that when I do this, somehow it gives me peace of mind. It feels like I'm putting the "bad" nonactionable things into a "time-out" list where I can safely ignore them for the time being.

Once we send pending items to the Waiting For list, our Trello organizer is nearly in full swing:

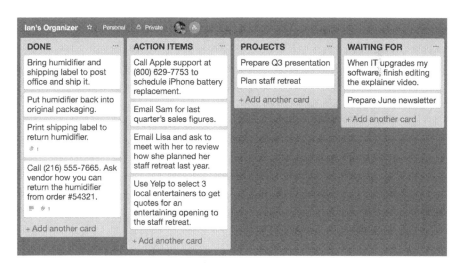

Move delayed tasks to the Waiting For list

Pretend your brain is a white board. Is it covered with to-do lists and "DO NOT ERASE"? Is there space for drawing and combining ideas?

—Jessica Kerr, software developer

Capture Mental Pop-Ups

This organizer isn't just for tasks that arrive over email. It's for what you volunteer to do in meetings, projects your supervisor assigns to you, and most certainly for ideas that keep popping up in your mind. Your brain will continually remind you of those good ideas until you get them out of your head and put them into your organizer. This brings us to the final list I recommend, which comes straight from the GTD system. It's the Someday/Maybe list. Use this to capture that amazing idea—for a new product, or a new way to save money, or a piece of office equipment you're considering buying—when you're too busy to really think about it in the moment. The more of these great ideas you can capture, the more you free your mind to think of even more good ideas! Now and then, you'll find yourself reviewing your Someday/Maybe list and pulling the best idea into the Projects list to start actively working on it. After storing these ideas in our Someday/Maybe repository, every list in our Trello organizer is now active and alive (see next page).

Once you have used your organizer for several days, you may find yourself slipping back into using your email as an organizer. If you're not checking the organizer and completing action items every day, you'll start to worry that something will slip between the cracks. You need to push yourself to use your organizer, and one sure-fire way to do that is to put vitally important things in there. Think about moving from one house or apartment to another. If you have a few days of overlap, where should you stay? The decision is quickly made when you realize that you're not sleeping anywhere your bed *isn't*. If you

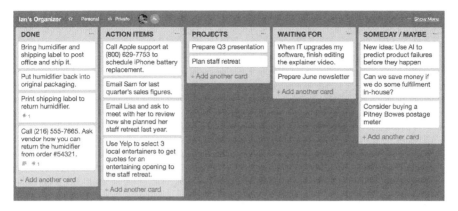

DONE	ACTION ITEMS	PROJECTS	WAITING FOR	SOMEDAY / MAYBE
Bring humidifier and shipping label to post office and ship it.	Call Apple support at (800) 629-7753 to schedule iPhone battery replacement.	Prepare Q3 presentation	When IT upgrades my software, finish editing the explainer video.	New idea: Use AI to predict product failures before they happen
Put humidifier back into original packaging.	Email Sam for last quarter's sales figures.	Plan staff retreat	Prepare June newsletter	Can we save money if we do some fulfillment in-house?
Print shipping label to return humidifier.	Email Lisa and ask to meet with her to review how she planned her staff retreat last year.	+ Add another card	+ Add another card	Consider buying a Pitney Bowes postage meter
Call (216) 555-7665. Ask vendor how you can return the humidifier from order #54321.	Use Yelp to select 3 local entertainers to get quotes for an entertaining opening to the staff retreat.			+ Add another card
+ Add another card	+ Add another card			

Save ideas for the future in the Someday/Maybe list

want to push yourself to stay in the new apartment, move your bed there. Similarly, if you want to push yourself to use your organizer, transfer important work into it so you have no choice but to check it.

Process Emails with the 4D Technique

Now that you have a functioning organizer, you can start processing every email in your inbox using the 4D technique: *do*, *delete*, *delegate*, and *defer*.

For each message, you need to decide whether to do it immediately, delete it if it's not actionable, delegate it to someone else, or defer it until later. It's an easy technique that is flexible enough to apply to every message in your inbox.

When you sit down to an inbox of unread messages, it's human nature to find the path of least resistance. You might scan the list of subject lines for a message that calls for a quick response. Once you've handled that, you might re-read the subject lines to find another easy one to check off your list, and so on. This is *checking* your email and not *finishing* it. If you find yourself looking at an email and thinking, *I'll handle this later*—stop. This is dangerous territory. It wastes a lot of time and prevents you from getting to zero. Follow the OHIO principle: only handle it once. You don't have to act immediately (we'll soon learn more about the deferring action), but don't handle the same email over and over again simply because you've allowed yourself to be distracted by an easier task. Be disciplined and process each email only once.

As we dive deeper into the 4D technique, one way to motivate yourself to really get to zero is to ask yourself: What kind of reputation would you rather have? Would you like your colleagues to view you as someone who sporadically replies to email, sometimes within a few minutes and sometimes after many days or weeks, or would you prefer to be trusted to respond to every email within one business day? New habits can be hard to form. Focusing on building your reputation can help you make the change.

Do Quick Tasks

If the email message is immediately actionable and it's going to take only a minute or two, just do it. This is David Allen's two-minute rule. The premise is that for a task that's really quick, it's faster and easier to just get it done than to log it into your organizer and return to it later. You can set the limit higher if you want, but it's supposed to be quick, so I wouldn't go much higher than about five minutes.

What falls in this category? If someone asks you for information that you have readily accessible or can quickly generate, just reply and you're done. Likewise, if someone wants to meet with you, reply with a link to your calendar and move on. If you have to decline, it's not going to get any easier tomorrow, so do it right away. Three sentences are all you need: "Thanks for your email. This is an interesting idea, but unfortunately due to my workload, I'm not able to meet about this. Sorry, and thank you for your understanding." On the other hand, if you do want to meet with the person, saying yes should be fast, too: "Sounds interesting. Let's start with a 15-minute phone meeting. Here's a link to my calendar." I like to start with 15 minutes so that people get to the point quickly. You can always schedule more time later if the conversation turns out to be worthwhile.

While we're talking about scheduling, if you really want to expedite the process, reply with a link to your calendar or some other way of making scheduling easy. Your colleague can pick an open slot, and the meeting will instantly appear on your calendar. You'll never have to endure the back-and-forth emails and the search for a date and time that works for both of you. Boomerang has a Gmail extension called Boomerang Calendar that does this, and there are dozens of alternatives, such as Doodle MeetMe, Vyte, YouCanBookMe, and Calendly. They all solve the same basic problem: those pesky scheduling emails. Watch the demo videos for those apps and see which one you want to try first, keeping in mind that some are only for scheduling meetings between you and another person, while others will let a group of people all chime in to select at a convenient time.

What else you can do efficiently in under two minutes? You can ask for more details on a request you received, make an introduction, send a link to driving directions and parking information, or give the go-ahead to make a purchase. As you practice the 4D technique, you will get very good at deciding whether a task is one you can truly do in just a few minutes or whether you should defer it until later.

Delete (Archive) Non-Actionable Messages

Research shows that approximately half of our email is not actionable: newsletters, announcements, auto-replies, and the long email chain on which you were copied for seemingly no reason. You can often tell just by looking at the subject line that these do not require your attention. These are the fastest to process. Just delete them.

I actually recommend archiving these messages instead of deleting so that they are not gone forever. Technically, deleted emails go into your trash folder, which is emptied periodically according to the policies of your organization or your email provider, so you do have a brief window of time in which to retrieve something you accidentally deleted. But once an email finally disappears from the trash folder, you can never get it back. Archiving, on the other hand, removes your messages from your inbox but retains them in case you need them later. The only situation in which I recommend actually deleting emails rather than archiving them is when you receive large email attachments and you're absolutely sure you won't need them again. Most organizations have a maximum storage capacity for each email account, and large unnecessary file attachments are the fastest way to find yourself over the limit.

Some of you may be using folders to archive your mail. I used to do this. I had a byzantine system of folders and subfolders so I could always find the message that I needed. This was a holdover from decades ago, when searching emails was slow. Today, searching is a much faster way to find what you're looking for than navigating a complex system of folders. I gave up on my hierarchical folder system in the year 2005. I found it difficult to make the switch, but as my email volume grew, I couldn't afford to spend the time thinking about where to put each and every email. Even if it takes only five seconds per message to decide the destination folder and then click and drag it there, that's ten minutes a day, or forty-two hours every year, that a person could spend merely organizing the average office professional's 121 daily email messages.

The beauty of archiving is it saves you time. Think of the archive folder as a reference library. One of the most powerful librarians in the world (your search tool) will instantly locate any item you need from your email. You can be confident that any item you put into this archive will be easy to retrieve.

If you're skeptical, consider this. In the early days of the internet when search engine capabilities were limited, we maintained carefully curated lists of all the websites we were likely to visit. Some of us stubbornly clung to those bookmarks while everyone else switched to using Google's search engine. Jump forward a few years, and even the most dedicated bookmarkers have realized that combing through long lists of bookmarks is an inefficient way to access the entire internet. Don't leave yourself stranded in the past. Get rid of those email folders, archive your emails as you process them, and be confident that you'll be able to find the emails you need using the search tool.

Delegate (Forward) If You're Not Responsible

Delegation is pretty straightforward: forward the message to the person who should take care of the action, then archive the original email.

There are a couple ways to handle this. You can forward the email to your colleague without copying the original sender. Maybe you want to add a private message for your colleague: "Hi, Sally. Here's a sales prospect, but be careful how you reply. He is prone to sending long, annoying emails about grammar and spelling." Be cautious with this approach, because it's easy for emails to spread further than you intended. Your colleague may accidentally forward the email chain back to the original sender, exposing what you've said. Also, it's not uncommon for emails to end up as courtroom evidence or to be reported in the news. Personally, I don't put anything in an email that would embarrass me if it were published on the front page of the *New York Times*.

Another method is to reply to the original sender and copy the colleague who's going to take care of the task. This is the classic technique: "Hi Mary, I'm forwarding your request to Ali on our communications team." You've replied to the sender, who now knows that your part in the email thread is over and that your colleague is going to take care of the request.

Here's a really good trick. If you want to make sure your colleague replies, the Boomerang app has a feature that does just that. Click the "Boomerang this" checkbox in your email, and if no one replies to the thread within a week (or whatever time frame you decide), the message will pop back up in your inbox so you can remind your colleague to respond. This is a great way to help ensure that loose ends get tied up.

One more pro tip. Move recipients to the bcc list as soon as possible. Have you ever forwarded an email to a colleague who forgot to take you off the cc list? It's annoying, and it wastes time to be flooded with emails that no longer pertain to you. If you want to demonstrate professional email etiquette, do this: Let's say your colleague Alice introduces you over email to Bob. Go ahead and reply, moving Alice to bcc, with a brief note saying, "Thanks, Alice (moved to bcc), and hi, Bob." This way, if Alice is keeping track, she knows you've responded. I first witnessed this "move to bcc" technique in 2012 when Paul Buchheit, the inventor of Gmail, introduced me to Michael Litt, the CEO of VidYard. I immediately saw the value in reducing the number of nonactionable emails that someone (Paul, in that case) would receive. Today, I am delighted when others politely move me to bcc.

Defer Time-Consuming Actionable Items

Defer is your final option when processing emails, when none of the other options apply. This is the least understood of the four Ds, and it's the step where things can go terribly wrong if you misunderstand what are you deferring and why. Defer does not mean leave the message in your inbox. Defer means you should move it to the organizer you created earlier in this book and archive the original email. If the VP asks you to prepare a presentation, put that on your Projects list. If the director of marketing and communications asks you to review a fact sheet for accuracy, script that out and put it into your Action Items list. Whatever you do, don't leave it in your email inbox. If you leave it there, you will never get to zero and never experience the feeling of being free from the distracting lure of email. This is critical, and I can't stress this enough. You will be tempted to leave a few emails in your inbox, and you might tell yourself that you're doing this because they are your top priority and you can't let these drop from your sight. After all, isn't inbox five good enough? Or maybe inbox fifty? All I can say is that this is a very slippery slope that will soon put you right back to where you started, using your email inbox as a shabby kind of organizer.

Let's bring learning the 4D technique to a close. To tackle your inbox, you do quick things right away, delete (archive) things that are not actionable, delegate items that belong in someone else's inbox, and defer longer tasks and projects to your organizer. The 4D technique is used by professionals all over the world. A Google search for "4D email management" shows thousands of web pages, videos, tutorials, diagrams, and blog posts on the topic. We're going to go beyond simply learning the technique, though, and witness the powerful psychological forces that really make it work.

The 4D Technique Simplifies Decision Making

Imagine there's a door you have to unlock, your office door, perhaps. You've forgotten your keys, and the custodian arrives with two key rings. One key ring is full of many individual keys, and each opens just one door. Let's say there are a hundred keys on this key ring, and it weighs several pounds. It's going to take you a long time to find the right key for your door. You might be more interested in the second key ring, which has four master keys. Even if you have to test out all four to find the one that works in your door, it's going to be much faster, right?

That's what we're doing with email. Email has become the place where all communication appears. In that everything box, we receive meeting invites, bank statements, app notifications, reminders to pick up someone at the airport, invitations to special events, advertising from brands, discussions about ongoing work projects, and updates from friends. With so many different kinds of content, if you handle each one differently, you'll spend a lot of time searching your mind for what action to take. If you can reduce the number of choices, like we reduced the number of keys in our example, you can make that choice much faster.

Let's look at the research to support this.

Fewer Choices Makes It Easier to Take Action

There's a common notion that the more options we have, the better off we are. We want more ice cream flavors. More cell phone providers. More people to choose from when we're dating. The assumption is that the more options there are, the closer we get to our perfect choice. It sounds reasonable. If there were just one style of jeans sold at a store and it's not one we like, then either we have to settle for an uncomfortable pair or we're without jeans. But if there were infinite options, we could find *exactly* the jeans we're looking for, right? This may sound logical, but in the real world, this leads to decision paralysis. As researchers have discovered, having a few options is advantageous—but that doesn't mean that more options are better.

These experiments have been conducted on all sorts of subjects, from chocolate to speed dating, but one of the most cited experiments took place in 1995 in a grocery store. Professor Sheena Iyengar at Columbia University and Professor Mark Lepper of Stanford University set up a free sample table and let customers sample varieties of jam. Sometimes there were just six flavors to choose from, and other times there were twenty-four flavors. Although more customers were lured in to try the jams at the table with a wider selection, the table with fewer jams resulted in more sales. How much more? With the larger assortment, 3 percent of customers purchased a jar, but with a smaller set to choose from, 30 percent bought a jar—that's ten times the sales! With fewer options, it was easier to make a decision.

Proctor and Gamble has used this knowledge. They reduced the varieties of Head & Shoulders shampoo from twenty-six to fifteen varieties and saw a 10 percent increase in sales. When the Golden Cat Corporation eliminated its ten worst-selling cat litter products, they saw an 87 percent increase in profits. At Apple, Steve Jobs pared the product portfolio down to just four computers when he resumed control of the company in 1997. Over the following ten years, the company's computer sales grew more than 800 percent.

This phenomenon has been shown in every field researchers have examined. Having just a few choices means it's easier to take action. We're taking advantage of this phenomenon with our email strategy. With just four options for how to process our email messages, it is easy to make the decision. Do, delete, delegate, or defer.

Be an Email Satisficer

Are you a maximizer, or are you a satisficer?

When you go to a restaurant, do you find yourself reading everything on the menu so you can choose the best possible meal, or do you go with the first thing that looks good? When you applied to college did you apply to dozens, or just a few? When you go clothes shopping, do you have a hard time deciding what to purchase?

The answers to these questions determine whether you a maximizer or a satisficer. The idea of maximizers and satisficers comes from the work of Nobel Prize-winning economist Herbert Simon, who created the notion of satisficer by combining the words *satisfying* and *sufficing*.

Maximizers want to make the absolute best decision. If they're searching for a new laptop, they won't make a decision until they've exhaustively reviewed every option so they know they are making the best possible choice. Even after they finally make a purchase, a maximizer may continue to read reviews of other laptops. Maximizers spend a lot of time and energy to reach a decision, and they're often anxious about whether they are, in fact, making the best choice.

Satisficers, on the other hand, review a modest number of options, quickly choose a good-enough option and move on to other tasks. It doesn't mean they have low standards—their standards may be just as high as the maximizer—but they have a defined set of criteria to test their selections against. As soon as they find the bicycle, hotel, or gift with the qualities they want, they end their search. In experiments, satisficers are typically happier with their decisions than maximizers, who continue to worry whether they have made the right choice. In *The Paradox of Choice*, psychologist Barry Schwartz even found data that satisficers tend to be happier people in general.

Schwartz advises that one way to fight the urge to maximize is to limit your choices. You might allow yourself to pick the best possible winter coat but force yourself to limit your selection to just one store instead of going from one store to another to another. That's what we're doing with the 4D technique. By limiting yourself to just these four choices, you are able to quickly make a good-enough decision in processing your email, of whether to do it, delegate it, delete it, or defer it, and get your inbox to zero.

Experience Inbox Zero for the First Time

> We who cut mere stones must always be envisioning cathedrals.
>
> —Medieval quarry worker's creed

Getting to inbox zero feels amazing. Archiving that very last email feels like climbing a mountain and getting the first glimpse of a boundless horizon. Like Hercules after completing his twelfth labor, you are suddenly free—of the enormous burden of email.

If you search on Twitter for inbox zero, you will see screenshots of empty inboxes posted by people bursting with pride. They post with hashtags like #AllCaughtUp, #BestFeeling, #CleanSlate, #LessStress, #GettingThingsDone, #Freedom, #Success.

Imagine having these feelings almost every hour of every day. If you pause your inbox, process to zero, and leave it paused, the feeling of being on top of your email never goes away. The point of this three-step system is to eliminate the feeling of email overload that has crept into our lives.

Drew Carey's Euphoria

One public figure who has been very open about his experience with inbox zero is comedian Drew Carey.

Besides being a humorous television personality, Drew Carey is also a voracious reader who focuses on constant self-improvement. He organizes dinner parties with thoughtfully crafted guest lists to bring bright minds together. As the host of perennial TV favorite *The Price is Right*, Carey often suggests books to his coworkers and has even paid for consultants to lead training sessions at the studio.

When battling his own information overload, he turned to David Allen, the creator of GTD, for help. Even with an assistant, Carey couldn't keep up with the voicemails, meetings, charity events to host, and daily avalanche of emails. After reading *Getting Things Done*, he knew he had found the right system to help him organize his life, and went so far as to fly Allen to his Hollywood home to help him implement the GTD system.

Allen sat with Carey, and for several days, they went through every email, voicemail, calendar reminder, and scribbled note. They even dove into Carey's mind to collect every single cognitive pop-up notification waiting to go off. Everything his mind had been tracking as undone went into Carey's new personal GTD system until he finally got to zero. Here's how he describes that moment, in an interview conducted by Roy Baumeister and John Tierney for their book *Willpower*:

> *Before, I'd see a pile of papers and wouldn't know what the hell was in them and [would] just be like, Oh, my God. The day I got to zero, which is GTD talk for having nothing in your inbox—no phone messages, no emails, nothing, not a piece of paper—when I got to that point, I felt like the world got lifted off my shoulders. I felt like I had just come out of meditating in the desert, not a care in the world. I just felt euphoric.*

With the need for his mental alerts gone, he was able to shift his focus to his true work, writing great comedy:

There's nothing worse than sitting down to write when you've got a blinking phone and a pile of letters and a ton of emails in your face. You're not going to do your very best work. But if you know the other stuff is taken care of, you can concentrate on your writing. You can be more creative.

For some reason, Drew Carey couldn't just ignore the less-important tasks and focus on writing comedy. Why is that the case? Is this just an anecdote of one person's experience, or have we uncovered a deep underlying feature of the human condition?

Free Your Mind of Unfinished Tasks

To a diligent person, every unfinished commitment clutters the mind with reminders to make good on unfulfilled promises. David Allen uses the term *open loops* to refer to these unfinished tasks. Every commitment you make to yourself or to others is an open loop that gets tracked by your psyche. These open loops become a sort of cognitive pop-up notification, interrupting you at random intervals throughout your day.

Psychologists have long had a name for this tension caused by unfinished tasks: the Zeigarnik effect, named after Bluma Zeigarnik, who studied this effect after witnessing a curious event in a French restaurant. A waiter had impressed her large table of psychologists by remembering each person's detailed order without writing it down. However, when a member of this group returned to the restaurant later to fetch a forgotten dinner jacket, not only had the waiter forgotten where they had sat or what they had eaten, the waiter didn't even recognize the person. How could someone with such a demonstrated capacity for memorization forget that information so quickly? The waiter explained that he remembered people and their orders only until they were served and no longer. This incident made an impression on Zeigarnik, who went on to demonstrate this effect in a lengthy series of experiments, eventually concluding that there is a tension in our minds surrounding unfinished tasks. The

Zeigarnik effect shows that our minds keep churning on something until we achieve closure, like a song that gets stuck in our head until we listen to it and get it out of our system. This is often used in the entertainment industry in the form of cliff-hangers so that you feel an intense need to watch the next episode in order to relieve the tension from the previous episode's suspenseful ending.

Modern researchers have discovered a way to short-circuit this effect. In the playfully titled study "Consider It Done," E. J. Masicampo and Roy Baumeister found that the tension of unfinished tasks will disappear if you simply write down a plan for taking care of it in the future. This is the same effect David Allen describes in *Getting Things Done*. The part of your mind that keeps reminding you to buy cat food or call your parents will quiet down if you form a plan of action to do those things at a later date. This could mean setting aside time on your calendar to do this, or adding it to your action items list, or using any other system that results in your mind being able to consider it done. You can clear your mind of the clutter of unfinished tasks just by writing a plan of action. Your mind will then stop pinging you with mental pop-up notifications.

This effect explains why using the 4D system with a proper organizer is so satisfying. For emails you can handle immediately using do, delete, or delegate, you eliminate those emails from your mind's list of unfinished tasks. For other tasks that you need to defer, you write them down in your organizer as action items or projects, at which point your mind considers it done. Either way, you win! When you get to zero, the cognitive burden of email will be gone.

The Freedom to Choose Your Focus

To the casual onlooker, mediation looks pretty easy: you sit, clear your mind, and breathe. Anyone can do it, and you don't need any special equipment. People who have actually tried meditating, however, will attest to what happens next. A chattering monkey appears in your mind, nagging you with a constant stream of thoughts: *Did*

> Most people have never tasted what it's like to have nothing on their mind except whatever they're doing.
>
> —David Allen

I send that email? . . . I should schedule a haircut before my presentation next week . . . I know I'm forgetting something. . . . For many of us, this nervous chattering appears when we least want it to, like when we're trying to get to sleep at night. Buddhists call this the monkey mind, jumping from one thought to the next as quickly as those long-tailed primates swing from tree to tree.

If the thought that you need to buy cat food keeps bouncing back and forth in your mind, that is your monkey mind being fearful that you will forget to take care of this task. By capturing that thought and converting it into an action plan, we know from Masicampo and Baumeister's research that the echo chamber in your mind will quiet down. If you can do this for all of the thoughts zipping around your mind, you will achieve a relaxed state that David Allen calls a "mind like water"—a peaceful state of mind where you respond to each new stimulus with just the right amount of focus. Envision yourself dropping a small pebble into a calm pond of water and witnessing the small ripple that results. If you instead were to drop a large stone, you would see a larger ripple. The pond's reaction is perfectly proportional to the size of the stone. In the analogy, a mind like water means reaching the point where trivial things take only a small amount of your focus, while large amounts of focus are reserved for dealing with the things that truly matter.

By quieting those internal alarms such as the compulsive need to check email, you achieve a state where you are free from distractions and free to choose where you invest your focused attention.

Leave it Paused

I f Newton were alive today, I imagine he would describe email like his third law of motion. For every email sent, there is an equal and opposite reply. One way to guarantee you receive more email is to send more to begin with. You send an email, which gets a reply, to which you send another reply, and so on in an endless chain reaction of emails throughout the day. By the time this

> For every action, there is an equal and opposite reaction.
>
> —Newton's third law of motion

game of electronic ping-pong has played itself out, what would have required a mere sixty-second phone call might instead have exploded into a dozen or more interruptions over email.

The opposite is surely true as well: the fewer emails you send, the fewer you'll receive. By pausing your inbox, you minimize how many times per day an email discussion can bounce back to you. And when your colleagues conduct discussions over email, you'll often be pleasantly surprised to see that a long email chain has resolved itself without your needing to be involved at all. Likewise, as your colleagues learn that you are not instantly available on email, they will begin to save discussions for regularly scheduled meetings and to use faster modes of communication for time-sensitive issues.

Meanwhile, with that pause button preventing interruptions, you can gleefully move forward on projects that have more impact and meaning.

Make the Most of Inbox Zero

This freedom to focus on what matters is the hidden gem of inbox zero. It's the reward that countless clickbait articles fail to see. The term *inbox zero* was first applied to email inboxes by time-management expert and founder of the productivity website 43Folders.com, Merlin Mann, and his purpose was not merely to keep things from falling between the cracks and to save time. It's no use saving time if you don't spend it wisely. Here is Mann in his own words: "It's about how to reclaim your email, your attention, and your life. That 'zero'? It's not how many messages are in your inbox—it's how much of your own brain is in that inbox. Especially when you don't want it to be. That's it."

So, onward curious readers, as we continue to devise an escape plan to rescue your brain from the tantalizing smorgasbord of distractions that is email, and beat ever forward towards deeply meaningful work.

What's Your MIT?

Let's do an exercise. You'll need something to write (or type) with. I'm going to ask you to think of three things. Are you ready? I want you to write down your three biggest priorities in life. Things like your health, friends, family, financial security, your partner, or your faith. Do you have it? Did you select your top three? Good.

Now for the reveal. Open your calendar and add up the hours each week that you spend on your three biggest priorities. For many of us, the number is staggeringly low, if not zero. We are self-aware enough to be able to list the things that mean the most to us, but when we look at how we allocate our time, we find they're just not there.

Time is a very interesting thing because it's the great equalizer. It doesn't matter who you are or how much money you have—each of us has twenty-four hours to spend in a day. Yet even when we know that our time is limited, we somehow manage to fill it with all sorts of commitments that don't reflect our priorities.

The same is true in our jobs. Think of your top three work priorities. They may be what will bring you recognition or what you're passionate about. They might include your most important projects or ongoing responsibilities. Often, though, when we look at our work calendars, they're filled with everything *except* our highest priorities.

Calendar events are meant to be commitments, the things we need to do, so block off time every day to work on your highest priorities. That can sometimes be difficult. If your primary goal is to maintain progress on a multiyear project, you can't just sit down and do that. Define a manageable chunk, something you will tackle today. This is your *most important task*, or MIT. Do this each day, and make consistent progress towards your largest and most important goals.

This is a concept that has taken on many different names. Leo Babauta of the popular blog *Zen Habits* also calls it your MIT, while real estate mogul Gary Kellar calls it your *one thing*, in a book of the same name. Time management coach Julie Morgenstern took a different approach in her book *Never Check Email in the Morning* (a subject we will soon cover).

Even Mark Twain, who would find it humorous to be included in a list of time management authors, had this to say about tackling your most important thing: "If it's your job to eat a frog, it's best to do it first thing in the morning. And if it's your job to eat two frogs, it's best to eat the biggest one first." As humans, we tend to avoid difficult work, even when it's the most important thing we have to do.

These authors all share a common theme: identify an achievable goal for the day and make it the first thing you do. They knew instinctively what researcher Roy Baumeister discovered in his laboratory, namely that willpower is strongest at the beginning of the day, and your daily quota of willpower decreases as the day progresses. Don't waste your most productive high-energy time on something as banal as email. Use that boost of morning willpower to tackle your MIT.

The point of the MIT solution (or whatever you want to call it) is to choose one thing you will do today, without fail, to make progress towards your larger goal. Your MIT will be different depending on your job. A start-up founder's MIT may be "create a new slide deck for Friday's pitch meeting," while a PhD candidate may choose to "add 500+ words to thesis," and a recent college graduate may "use Indeed.com to find three job openings to apply to." Whatever you choose, make it important, make it achievable, and get it done.

Stay Focused and Out of Email

Your inbox is now empty, and it will be empty for as long as you keep it paused. You can no longer procrastinate on difficult high-value tasks by jumping back into your email and checking off a handful of easy, low-value tasks. It's time to tackle your MIT and make progress on the challenging projects you'll look back on with pride.

Unfortunately, for most of us, it's just not that easy. Even with an empty inbox, you will probably still find it hard to focus. You may find yourself giving in to other distractions. Perhaps it's stopping by a colleague's office just to say hi or countless trips to the coffee machine. We want to believe that once we eliminate the sources of distraction, we'll have laser-like focus on the work in front of us. Instead, we find ourselves falling prey to the unfortunate human tendency to avoid difficult tasks. Beyond that, focusing on work is made even harder by the constant distractions of modern technology. When we're supposed to be drafting an action plan for a high-value business opportunity, we find ourselves on YouTube watching videos. We go on Facebook just to quickly message a friend; several hours later, our minds snap back into reality from a media-induced time vortex. The next time you're in line at a coffee shop or grocery store, take a look at the other people in the line. How many are alone and *not* on their phone? Most of us can't endure silence or stillness for even brief periods. We immediately take out our smartphone and become absorbed in its many distractions.

One of the foremost experts on how technology is impacting humans was the late Stanford professor Clifford Nass. In a 2009 study, Nass and coauthors Eyal Ophir and Anthony D. Wagner explained that nearly everyone has the same amount of attention to allocate. It's where we allocate it that makes a difference. Nass lived alongside students as a dorm parent and saw them texting, talking, watching TV, and doing homework—all simultaneously. At first, he was impressed, thinking these students had developed an amazing cognitive ability to focus on multiple tasks. But when he tried to find proof for this in his research, he instead found that the more the students multitasked, the less productive they were and the less they could focus when they wanted to.

What's amazing is that chronic multitaskers don't realize this— they think multitasking makes them more productive and that they can still focus when they need to. They insisted to the researchers that even though their typical way of working was to constantly switch between tasks, when they really needed to concentrate, they could be "laser-focused." But what the research team actually found was that the multitaskers had developed habits of mind that made focused concentration impossible. They were "suckers for irrelevancy" who "just can't keep on task."

Focus is not the lack of distractions; it's the ability to ignore them. It takes willpower to focus, because you need to ignore short-term temptations (like that YouTube video someone shared of cats playing the piano) in favor of long-term goals (like finishing the presentation that's due next Friday). If we have lost some of our willpower to focus, the good news is that we might be able to get it back. Willpower is like a muscle, and for many of us, it has atrophied with the advent of the smartphone. But also like a muscle, we can build it through exercise.

So, how do we strengthen this part of the brain? How do we filter out distractions and turn our brains into laser-focused cognitive machines?

Rebuild Your Brain's Focus

Email is an extremely tempting form of distraction, but there are powerful strategies that will come to our aid in resisting it. Try these techniques to fortify your brain's ability to achieve sustained focus.

1. Use an Implementation Intention

    Arguably one of the most powerful strategies in modern psychology's toolbelt is implementation intention. This is a self-regulatory strategy for controlling our behaviors, and it often takes the form of an if-then plan. With a generic intention like "eat healthy," the research shows a weak link between intentions and actions. It just doesn't do much to change our behaviors. But by formulating the intention as a specific if-then implementation plan, "If I go out to eat, then I will get a salad," these plans have significantly higher success rates for just about every goal we can think of, from dieting to using public transportation more frequently to avoiding prejudicial thoughts. Peter Gollwitzer, a researcher at New York University, showed that participants who repeated these if-then phrases to themselves three times were two to three times more likely to succeed. In one study, 91 percent of people who used an if-then plan stuck to an exercise program, versus the 39 percent who didn't. Researchers are perplexed by this, because it goes completely against the traditional understanding of how we form habits. Normally, we develop a habit through repetition over an extended period, but with an if-then plan, we act according to these plans as if we had carefully built a habit over months or years. It's an incredible shortcut, and strangely, it works independently of our willpower, so even at the end of the day when our willpower is depleted, we are somehow able to follow through on these intentions. These plans become wired as an automatic response, outside our rational thinking. It's as if our subconscious minds are keeping us on autopilot.

Modern psychology is incredibly excited about the strange power of these if-then implementation intentions, and we can use them to rebuild our focus. If you have added time for your MIT to your calendar and want to make sure you don't get distracted, try silently reading the statement below three times and then say it out loud to yourself one more time.

> *If I am scheduled to do my MIT, then I will tell myself I'm not allowed to do anything else.*

You've really done this, right? Be honest, now. For this book to be truly useful, you'll need test the exercises for yourself.

When your scheduled time slot arrives to do your MIT, if you feel tempted to unpause your email or to get lost in your smartphone, your subconscious will remind you that you're not allowed. You are allowed to work on your MIT only. Not only will you be accomplishing your goal for the day, but you'll also be exercising your mind's ability to focus.

2. Use a "Bright Line"

Research on email is clear that checking email less frequently reduces stress. We may say we want to do that, but what does "less frequently" really look like? Will we just "try to be better about it" and hope that works? Many a New Year's resolution to "lose weight" or "spend more time with friends" fails because these promises are too vague. On a daily basis, we can ignore them without really breaking a promise we made to ourselves. A real commitment is something you can measure. It's a clearly defined bright red line that you can't possibly cross without knowing that you've lied to yourself. Bright lines are statements like these:

I will no longer eat croissants, ever.

I will no longer drink sugary beverages, except for pure fruit juice and no more than one per day.

I will block off every Sunday morning from 11 a.m. to 1 p.m. for brunch with friends. If no friends are available, I will use that time to call friends who are far away.

If we make a clear and unbending contract with ourselves, we send a strong message to our subconscious: we will do this, or we will have lied to ourselves. It completely eliminates the wiggle room that you find in a typical resolution. So, if you want to stay out of email, try making one of these agreements with yourself:

I will unpause email only once a day, never more.

I will never unpause my work email on a day I am not working.

These bright lines are powerful because they change the conversation in your head from something you're giving up (sugary drinks) to something you're gaining: self-empowerment. With a bright line in place, you are merely following an identity that you have invented for yourself. You can simply tell others, "No thanks, I can't have sugary drinks." It's very empowering to know that you are becoming the kind of person that you've identified you want to be.

3. Delay Gratification

There is perhaps no lens more potent to focus your willpower than delayed gratification.

I can meet my friends for ice cream only after I finish these staff reviews.

Before I will let myself get lunch, I need to schedule that doctor's appointment I've been putting off.

I can watch an episode of Dr. Who *only if I finish my statistics homework.*

Boomerang's blue Unpause button is very tempting to click. One way to use delayed gratification here is to tell yourself that you can unpause only after you've processed every single email out of your inbox. You know, the ones you really don't want to deal with but that you absolutely must? I'm talking about those really sticky emails that seem to cling to our inboxes like super glue. If you unpause without processing those, if that is your habit, then very quickly you will find yourself with an inbox full of tasks you've put off dealing with. You're trying to get to inbox zero, not inbox one thousand. Don't let yourself unpause until you've forced yourself to deal with every single email in there.

4. Quantify Your Progress

We can learn a thing or two about resisting temptation from people who are successfully battling addictive substances. There is a saying in Alcoholics Anonymous: If you don't want to slip, don't go where it's slippery. Don't open up social media or unpause your email when you are focusing. It may be tempting to think that we can just take a quick look, but we must resist this temptation. If we're honest with ourselves, we know what really happens when we indulge in a "quick" look.

The sober crowd monitors their progress at avoiding the slippery slope. They use sobriety calculators to track the number of days since their last alcoholic drink because it builds momentum for remaining sober. Seeing your number grow builds your confidence.

Wearable fitness devices like Fitbit similarly build a sense of accomplishment towards our health goals. They visually show our progress and turn our modest daily achievements into a sort of game.

Quantifying and monitoring our behaviors can also help us stay out of email. I use a free desktop app called RescueTime, which automatically tracks how many minutes and hours I've spent on email. By monitoring my progress in reducing my email time, I was able to cut my email time from six hours a day to under an hour (a daily average of just under fifty-three minutes as of this writing).

Do Emails at the End of the Day

Save your emails for the end of the day, when your willpower is depleted and you need the fast reward of some easy tasks to check off.

Before we go any further on this topic, we must first tell the story of the famous marshmallow experiment. This is easily the most well-known study that will come up in any discussion of willpower. Conducted by Stanford professor Walter Mischel more than fifty years ago, this experiment explored self-control in children with a mischievous test that laid the groundwork for our modern understanding of self-control. In his lab, Mischel presented young children with a plate of marshmallows and gave them a simple choice.

They could eat one marshmallow as soon as they wanted, or if they waited a few minutes for the researcher to return, they could have two marshmallows. The experimenter would then leave the room for fifteen minutes and secretly observe through a camera feed as the children attempted to muster the willpower needed to not eat the tantalizing treat placed directly in front of them.

There is a popular YouTube video recreating this famous experiment, and it's hard not to laugh while watching these children attempt everything they could think of to avoid eating the marshmallow. Some turned away from the marshmallow or sang songs. Others distracted themselves by kicking their legs or drumming on their heads. They would smell the marshmallow repeatedly and even kiss it. Several children dramatically grabbed at the marshmallow and placed it halfway into their mouths, only to regain self-control a split second later and set the marshmallow down with a sigh. Some took tiny bites they thought would be imperceptible to the experimenter. If you need a feel-good mental break, visit the link to this video found in the notes at the end of this book.

Over 600 children took part in the original 1960 experiment. A small number of children immediately ate the marshmallow, and only a third of those who attempted to wait were successful in delaying gratification long enough to earn the second marshmallow. At the time, this represented a novel way of measuring willpower, but the incredible impact of the experiment continued to ripple throughout the field of psychology years later, when Mischel revisited his marshmallow eaters in their teenage years. He found that the participants who had waited longer for the marshmallows as preschoolers scored around 200 points higher on the SAT and that their parents were more likely to rate them as having a greater ability to plan, handle stress, respond to reason, exhibit self-control in frustrating situations, and concentrate without becoming distracted. The effects were even more pronounced when another researcher tracked down the original subjects decades later, when they were in their 40s. Amazingly, their self-control held up over four decades, and the ones who demonstrated willpower earlier in life now had better health and lower stress, and were happier than their counterparts who could not delay gratification.

Another groundbreaking discovery came in the early 2000s when Roy Baumeister finished a series of experiments that showed the concept of willpower fit a particular pattern. It all started with chocolate and radishes. Baumeister brought subjects into a room filled with the delicious aroma of freshly baked chocolate chip cookies. The participants were asked to sit at a table on which there was a plate of cookies and a bowl of radishes. Some were asked to sample the cookies, while others were forbidden from tasting the cookies and asked to sample the radishes. Next, they were given thirty minutes to complete a difficult geometric puzzle—a popular research technique to measure willpower. Baumeister and his colleagues found the people who were asked to resist the enticing cookies and eat only radishes gave up on the puzzle after about eight minutes, while the more fortunate cookie eaters continued working on the puzzle for nearly nineteen minutes, on average. Resisting the temptation of the freshly baked cookies seemed to drain the subjects of self-control. Subsequent experiments continued to reinforce the idea that you start each morning with a quota of willpower that is depleted as you use it throughout your day.

Think of the battery icon on your smartphone and how the bar slowly drains throughout the day. This is your willpower. When your self-control bar is at 100 percent, you can resist almost any temptation and push yourself to do almost anything. Throughout your day, however, that bar shrinks as you make decisions, push yourself to finish important work, and get through stressful or frustrating meetings and conversations. At the end of the day, when your bar is dangerously low, this is not the time to tackle your MIT. Instead, this is the time to finally unpause that inbox and let yourself experience the gratification of seeing replies you've been waiting for. With your MIT already finished, go ahead and process everything in your inbox. The joy of seeing your inbox back at zero is a wonderful feeling to cap off your day.

So don't do emails in the morning. Do your MIT first and save emails for the end of your day. This isn't a hard-and-fast rule. If your job requires you to have faster than one-day turnaround on issues, you may need to do more than one batch of emails a day. In that case, think about doing two batches—one batch before lunch and one later in the afternoon. Whatever you do, though, don't start your day with emails or you've lost the golden hour of highest productivity that you could have spent on career-defining initiatives.

Set New Expectations

> For anything to change, someone has to start acting differently.
>
> —Chip and Dan Heath, authors of multiple New York Times bestsellers, including *Switch* and *Made to Stick*

Before I developed this system for condensing email time into one efficient daily batch, I was compulsively checking my email at all times of the day. I had a sad, misplaced sense of pride surrounding how quickly I could reply to an email. I would check my email even while in bed, and when I received an email at 11:05 p.m. and sent a response by 11:10 p.m., somehow, that made me feel important. I felt like an all-powerful email genie with a magically fast response time. In my mind, this was sending the message to colleagues and folks higher up the ladder that I was a person who was intensely organized and fiercely on top of things. Indeed, I was sending a message, but by the time I realized what it was, it was too late.

Over the course of several years, my bad habits had taught the people who work with me three things:

1. I am always on email.
2. I have no boundary between work and personal life.
3. I have nothing more important to do.

At that point in my life, I was following every business lead, no matter how insignificant. I was responding to the most trifling request with a three-page action plan. I immediately agreed to every request made of my time, and in those rare instances when I needed to say no, I would put it off because I didn't want to deal with the discomfort.

Eventually, I realized the hole I had dug for myself. I had taught my colleagues to expect lightning-fast responses, and they liked knowing that I would drop everything the instant they needed some tidbit of information. When I gathered the courage to set better boundaries, people were understandably confused, and it took some time for them to adjust.

How can you help the people you work with understand your new email habit?

First and foremost, anticipate some resistance. As humans, we resist change, because we focus more on what we have to give up than what we have to gain. Psychologists have long known of this effect. They know we stare longer at negative photographs. We buy more newspapers when the headlines make us angry. We are more upset about losing $50 than we are happy about gaining $50. Even our language is more negative than positive: an analysis of 558 emotional root words in English found 62 percent of them were negative while only 38 percent were positive. This is true in other languages as well. A researcher studying marriages found that couples were likely to stay together only if there were five times as many positive events as negative ones. When researchers attempted to find the limits of our negativity bias, their depressing conclusion was that with few exceptions, bad is stronger than good.

Your coworkers are likely no different than the rest of us. When they notice that you are not replying to emails quite as fast as you used to, they will need to hear enough significant benefits that, from their perspective, outweigh the negatives. Any leader who has brought change to an organization is well aware of the stubborn resistance that can be encountered when trying to introduce an innovation or shift deeply engrained habits. Many best-selling books are dedicated to the topic of change management, and in the following sections, we will apply the best of those strategies to help the people you work with understand and embrace this change, and perhaps even try it for themselves.

Communicate Your New Email Policy

Of all the problems today's leaders face, a shortage of books on leadership is not one of them. As we consider how to communicate your new productivity habits to your colleagues, a mountain of articles, books, online courses, and talks on the topic of change management will aid us in this process. When an organization is faced with large-scale change, consultants will often advise its leader to communicate the change frequently and early, to offer listening sessions that provide opportunities for feedback, to find early adopters to test and debug a new system, and so forth. It's a lot of work. Fortunately, the scope of our challenge is not that vast. Our objective is simply to communicate to your colleagues that for truly urgent situations, they should stop using email and use a faster communication method.

On one hand, this should be obvious. Given the immediate availability provided by cell phones and text messaging (not to mention the benefits of simply getting someone's attention in person), why would anyone choose email when it is arguably the slowest available method of professional communication? And yet there we are, sending emails regarding crucial time-sensitive issues. I did this myself before starting down the path to inbox zero.

It's clear that there will be a small change to guide your colleagues through. If you can set great expectations and then deliver, you will be well on your way to a successful change. You can couple this with an advanced change management tactic for really effective results. For example, you can shrink the resistance you'll encounter if your team sees it not as a permanent change but merely as a temporary inconvenience. When we think a big permanent change is coming, our defensive shields go up. If we believe instead that the change is only for a trial period and that our feedback will be considered before implementation, it tends to bring out our intellectual curiosity. Consider using the following template when you email your colleagues about your new habit.

Dear colleagues,

I want to ask for your support on a new productivity habit I'm trying called inbox zero. The goal is to process emails more efficiently so I can spend more time engaging in deeply valuable work for our organization.

Over the next month, I would like to test this out by devoting the first few hours of each work day to making significant progress on important long-term projects. Because of this, I'd like to restrict my daily email time to 3:00–5:00 p.m. This will be a one-month trial.

What this means is that next month, I'll be less instantly available over email. I promise to read and respond to all email messages within one business day. For urgent matters I humbly ask you to call, text, or find me in person. For critical time-sensitive issues, I will always make myself available to you.

Many thanks in advance for your support and encouragement.

Emailing this to your colleagues can also serve a second purpose. By declaring your intention publicly, it can help you commit to your new habit. Your colleagues can double as accountability partners as they ask you how inbox zero is working. You are thus pressured to make good on your public promise of really trying out this new productivity habit.

If it makes you feel anxious to imagine sending this email or if you are worried about what your colleagues may say, you can take a subtler approach by changing your habit without announcing it. If you opt for this, consider putting your personal email policy in your email signature to slowly spread the message. Here's mine:

Email Policy

I respond to all emails within one business day. For urgent issues, please call.

Stay on Message

Do you ever wonder why Coke and Pepsi still put money into advertising? Throughout my travels, I have yet to meet a person who is not familiar with these products, and yet their billboards seem to be everywhere. I struggle to imagine someone seeing the billboard and turning to a friend for explanation. "Wow, Sam, you've really never had a soda? I'll take you to the store right away!" This scenario is not why they pay for those billboards.

Messages are more effective when they are repeated. We remember phrases like "What happens in Vegas stays in Vegas" (first appearance: 2004) or "Good to the last drop" (first appearance: 1917) because we've heard them again and again.

Given this insight, it should not surprise us that we will need to gently remind our coworkers for some time before they are accustomed to the new habit. When someone asks me, "I emailed you an hour ago. Why haven't you replied?!" I take a deep breath so I can reply calmly, "I try not to be instantly available on email. I need some of my workday to be uninterrupted for work that requires a lot of focus."

I might remind them that I respond to all emails within one business day, and if they need something faster, they can get my attention instantly over the phone or in person. If I have a good working relationship with the person, I might gently chide them by asking, "This seems urgent. Is email the best way to communicate urgent issues?"

Stay on message, as they say in the marketing world, and prepare yourself to repeat it whenever the topic comes up. There are infinite variations:

I do emails between 3:00 and 5:00 p.m. each day.

You can count on me for a response within one business day for every email. If you need something faster, you can always call or text.

The challenge to email is that truly urgent things can get buried under 200 nonurgent things. It's best to pick up the phone for things that are time sensitive.

There is a slippery slope with email. It used to be that a one-week turnaround time was fine, then one day. Now some managers will blow up if you don't reply in five minutes, it's crazy. If we don't collectively agree to change this, it will just keep getting worse.

If you have a coworker who constantly seems to be coming to you at the last possible minute, it might be time to give them a little unsolicited career advice. Ask them, "How did this become urgent?" or "When did you first get this assignment?" Let them know that you like them and you want to see them succeed, but you've noticed that they often let things become urgent and you're worried it could create a reputation for them as unorganized. Ask them if they can change that for the next time.

I find that it's often the less organized people who create these unnecessary crises. Although we may be tempted to put up a curt poster expressing, "A lack of planning on your part does not constitute an emergency on mine," consider instead the idea of gifting them a copy of this book or of *Getting Things Done*. Let them know what you personally found valuable about it and that you think they may enjoy it.

At this point in my life, I have sent and received over half a million emails, but I don't let it control me. I get to choose where I invest my focused attention, and I choose to focus on the vitally important. You can, too, if you decide to make yourself less instantly available. If you're still not convinced, think about this: if you emailed a truly important person at your organization, would you expect a five-minute turnaround time on email? Probably not. You know that person is doing wildly valuable things. So what does that say about the person who *is* responding within five minutes? Do you want to be known as someone who responds to emails quickly or someone who rigorously delivers on project after project of immense value? By opting for the latter, you fulfill a deep human need for purpose.

Accomplish Remarkable Things

The success of Apple is often attributed to Steve Jobs's visionary business leadership, but engineers are quick to point out that Jobs would have had nothing to sell without Steve Wozniak. The Woz, as he is affectionately known, is a legendary figure in the history of the modern computer. He created the very first Apple I computer just for fun—to share with the Homebrew Computer Club. This was an informal group of early hardware hackers who gathered to trade parts and circuits and to show off their latest inventions. From their ranks came the founders of many early microcomputer companies, and for this reason, the club is thought by many to be one of the single most influential forces in the formation of Silicon Valley's culture.

> Things which matter most must never be at the mercy of things which matter least.
>
> —Goethe

When prompted, the Woz is happy to share stories about his inventions. I had the fortune to meet him when he visited the innovation center I manage at Case Western Reserve University, and I heard firsthand about the hours he spent designing and redesigning his products. Like a marathon runner, he would be unwavering in his focus, working long stretches late into the night and starting again the moment he woke the next morning. When he finished a design, he would often tear it up and start over if he was struck with a clever insight for making a circuit design more elegant. This fanaticism almost single-handedly birthed Apple Computer.

At the time, Wozniak was being paid very little for his work. Jobs was known for taking a disproportionate share of the profits, considering how much less time he spent working compared with Wozniak. In interviews, though, the Woz insists that compensation was far from his main concern: "I just loved going down to Homebrew Computer Club, showing off my ideas, and designing neat computers. I was willing to do that for free for the rest of my life." He was driven by the insatiable urge to create. This is the kernel of truth that we will now explore.

The story of Steve Wozniak is not at all singular. Bill Gates was known for similarly obsessive stints of software programming in the early days of Microsoft. Ron "Typewriter" Mingo, who holds three world records for typing speed (this after a career in professional baseball and football), says the motivation came from himself—simply from wanting to be the best. Marie Curie was known for her indomitable work ethic, neglecting to eat and then falling asleep in her lab in order to gain just a few more minutes of research time.

We may not win a Nobel prize like Marie Curie, but we have something special in common with her. When properly motivated, our work can enthrall us. It can bring us so much joy that we forget to eat and sleep. But what is that secret motivator?

Perhaps no researcher on human motivation is cited more often than Frederick Herzberg. His 1968 publication "One More Time: How Do You Motivate Employees?" sold 1.2 million reprints in its first two decades and became the most requested article of its era from the *Harvard Business Review*. It puts forward an idea that managers now call the two-factor theory of work motivation, which defines "motiva-tor factors" separately from what he called "hygiene factors."

Hygiene factors include feeling safe at work, respecting and be-ing respected by your colleagues, and receiving an appropriate salary. If those factors are missing or in poor shape, we feel dissatisfied at work. But interestingly, the presence of these does not lead to mo-tivation. It merely predicts a lack of dissatisfaction. You can be se-verely demotivated if you don't feel safe at work. Yet if you *do* feel safe, chances are you don't notice this on a daily basis. Instead, you think that is normal and to be expected.

Motivator factors, on the other hand, are things like being al-lowed to achieve and being recognized for those achievements, being trusted with greater responsibility, having more involvement in orga-nizational decision making, and engaging in meaningful work. With a sense of achievement, progress, recognition, and personal growth, people report they feel like there's no such thing as arriving too early or staying too late—their enjoyment of the job simply has no end.

This finding has been replicated by scores of researchers. Te-resa Amabile and Steven Kramer from Harvard University analyzed 12,000 diary entries of corporate employees to find that the feeling of progress and achievement, not pay incentives, was the biggest mo-tivator. Cal Newport of Georgetown University, in his popular book *Deep Work*, described the intrinsic and extrinsic benefits of focusing without distraction on a cognitively demanding task. Hungarian re-searcher Mihály Csíkszentmihályi (pronounced cheek-sent-me-high) recognized and named the psychological concept of *flow*, a highly fo-cused mental state, in his book of the same name. Daniel Pink in his book *Drive* argues the secret to motivating ourselves is to connect with the deeply human needs for autonomy, mastery, and purpose. Researchers have found time and time again that human satisfaction is deeply tied to our ability to achieve progress on meaningful work. This is not surprising. Sophisticated readers devour books like *Deep Work*, *Flow*, and *Drive* because they confirm something that we want and instinctively know to be true—that our lives are more than a series of trivial assignments. We are capable of greater heights than a hastily sent email composed while munching on lunch at our desks.

Conclusion

I hope this book confirmed the suspicion you've had all along, that email is taking our time away from real work. Every time we attempt to focus on something truly important, email is ready to bombard us with a constant stream of interruptions. With new technology like Boomerang, along with a renewed commitment to focus on deep work, we are able to freeze those attention-snagging beeps, buzzes, and pop-ups before they can get to us.

The science-based strategy presented in this book will keep your inbox empty for most of the day. Starting each morning with an empty inbox, you'll be able to focus on your most important thing for the day so you can be sure that no matter what else happens that day, you've completed something that's important to you. Later each afternoon, you'll unpause your inbox and process your email for the day using the 4D technique along with your organizer to capture and script out your work. Planning the rest of your day is up to you. Whether you fill that time with meetings or schedule more time for deep work will depend on the type of job you have and what your goals are.

My personal definition of a good day at work is when I've made visible progress on long-term goals, emptied my inbox, and managed to not take any work home with me. With more days like that, you'll have more time for things that are truly important to you—both at work and in your personal life. As you've no doubt realized, the point of this book is not to get more email done, it's to get more life done. Empty your inbox, turn off your computer, and go live your life.

Expert Mode

Productivity geeks are always eager (usually too eager) to share their solutions, and I am no exception. If you liked the tips and tricks in this book, such as using Boomerang to make sure nothing falls between the cracks, or using Trello to set up your organizer, here are some additional ideas to consider adding to your repertoire.

Strategies for Difficult Emails

The 4D processing technique is even more effective when it's complemented by a set of general-purpose strategies for tackling the difficult emails that frustrate our attempts to clear our inbox. You know the kind—you open it and think, *What on earth am I going to do with this one?* Maybe it's a new partnership opportunity, but you're not sure if it's going to be worth it. Maybe someone has invited you to speak at a conference, but you're considering taking a vacation that week and haven't decided yet. Maybe it's an angry email from your colleague, or a performance complaint about someone on your team. It could just be something you want to decline, but you're having trouble finding the right words to say no without feeling guilty. Some emails are just really hard to deal with. It would be great if we had a wizard of difficult situations hiding in a corner of our offices, whispering amazing solutions. Our own personal Cyrano, quietly advising us from under our desks. Let's go over some general purpose strategies to help deal with the variety of things that end up in our email inboxes.

Ask a Clarifying Question

Many situations can be handled skillfully by asking thoughtful clarifying questions.

Ask for more details on what the person saw, or what's needed in response, or what length and format it should be. Ask if there is a deadline and what level of quality is needed at this stage. Ask for a brief background on the incident or whether anyone else saw it. Ask for any data on the scenario or what the person sees as possible options and the pros and cons. Ask if the situation has happened in the past and, if so, how often and how others have dealt with this.

Asking clarifying questions puts the ball back in the other person's court, without you needing to have a complete answer or solution. You can use this when you really do need more information, or you can use it when you don't have a solution yet, but you want to provide a response that keeps the conversation going. This is very versatile tactic that can be applied to many different situations.

Make a Good-Enough Decision

Some of the most difficult emails to process are the ones where you need to make a decision where there is no perfect answer. It could be a business opportunity that has equal numbers of pros and cons, or maybe you are being asked to choose between two positive options with no clear winner.

In these situations, it's easy to follow the path of least resistance and give in to the temptation to find an easier email to handle. Of course, this does not work as a strategy for actually dealing with these situations. Avoid the path of least resistance and force yourself to make a good-enough decision. Here are a few tips.

When it comes to business opportunities, there's a saying that if it's not a "Hell yes!" then it's a no. Don't let mediocre options absorb your time. Say no right away, and preserve your time for opportunities that have tremendous potential.

When it comes to selecting options from a very long list, be careful of the curse of having too many options. Remember Professors Iyengar and Lepper's jam experiment. The people who saw fewer flavors were ten times as likely to actually buy jam. You can artificially limit your selections to make it more likely that you'll actually decide. Instead of looking at hundreds of options, limit yourself to just the first page of search results.

When it comes to selecting between options that look equally good, give yourself permission to make an arbitrary decision. Decide that you will always select the option on the left, or flip a coin, or use some other strategy that will get you to a decision you can live with and allow you to move on.

As a last-ditch strategy, try sleeping on it but just for one night. In the morning, if you don't have any new feelings about it, admit to yourself from your own experience that adding another day, or seven days, or a month, isn't going to help. Don't procrastinate. Make a good-enough decision and get on with it.

Take It Off-Line

Talking, it turns out, is a very efficient way to communicate. We average around 150 words per minute when we're in a conversation. Compare that to typing, which has an average speed of only around 45 words per minute. We can see that talking on the phone is more than three times faster than typing the same message. For longer discussions or ones involving numerous people, you might arrange a meeting, but for quick questions or issues, try picking up the phone.

For some of us, this may seem counterintuitive—and here's where things get interesting. Some of us prefer to communicate over email because it somehow feels faster. We may have a voicemail greeting that directs callers to email us instead of leaving a voice message. If you have ever felt this way and wondered why, there's a very good reason. We can read far faster than we can type or even talk—at a staggering rate of 280 words per minute. That's only an average, so perhaps you can read even faster. Reading is simply the fastest way to get information into your brain. It's almost twice as fast as hearing someone talk. So it's great for you, the reader, because you can get through it more quickly than any other medium in the modern workplace. But what is that like for the person who has to type that message to you? On average, that person is capable of transmitting emails to you at only 45 words per minute. So selfishly asking people to send emails makes *us* faster, but we ought to consider what that does to our colleagues and to our team's overall efficiency.

In a hypothetical 200-word communication that involves you and another person each transmitting and receiving 100 words, it will take 309 seconds using email but only 80 seconds in a verbal discussion. That's 386 percent faster. I can imagine the clickbait now: "Ohioan discovers amazing app that cuts communication time by 386 percent!"—and when you click on this you see that the secret app is called the telephone.

Beyond the issue of speed, when people can hear your voice, they know a lot more about your intentions because they can hear your tone. In email, you aren't really sure if someone is being sarcastic or sympathetic, because vocal tone and nonverbal communication cues have been eliminated. Author and computer scientist Cal Newport puts it this way: "Synchronous conversation is efficient and nuanced. Not only does it allow you to handle in three minutes decisions that might have otherwise taken three days of attention-snagging messages, but it tends to also produce more thoughtful conclusions."

Boomerang It

Some of the messages that clog our inboxes are ones we can't act on because we're waiting for something. You might be waiting for a certain calendar date. You could be waiting until after a conference is over to give feedback on a colleague's talk or waiting until a press embargo is lifted before thanking a donor for a generous contribution. Perhaps instead you're waiting on someone to reply to a message you sent. Maybe it's a sales quote you requested from a vendor, or information you need for a monthly newsletter, or a client who hasn't paid their bill yet. If you're a conscientious person, you know that sometimes people don't reply, and you need a way to prevent things from falling between the cracks. In any case, you're waiting for something to happen before you can archive an email.

If you keep these pending emails in your inbox, you'll never get to zero. Worse, you'll waste time reading them over and over again as you process your email, each time remembering that you can't take action. Instead, remember the OHIO (only handle it once) rule and get those emails out of your inbox until the right time arrives to deal with them.

If you're very clear on your next actionable step, then you don't need to invest the time scripting and adding this to the Waiting For list in your organizer. Instead, you can use the Boomerang app to schedule a time for the message to reappear in your inbox. With the app installed, when you're sending a message you will see a new checkbox you can click to tell Boomerang to bring this back to your inbox if nobody responds. The date is configurable, so you can Boomerang the message in two hours, in one week, or on a specific date in a few months, whatever is appropriate for the situation.

You can also use Boomerang to eliminate any message that's already in your inbox and schedule its return for whenever you'll be ready to take action on it. For example, if you see a message in your inbox that doesn't need follow-up until the next fiscal quarter, open it and click the Boomerang icon, and set it to return at the beginning of the next quarter. The message will disappear from your inbox and reappear at just the right time.

One more pro tip. Boomerang also has a feature called Send Later that allows you to schedule your outgoing emails. You can now stop creating calendar reminders to send future emails. Just write the email now, and tell Boomerang to send it later. You can use this to send reminders to yourself or to others. You can also use it to make your email appear in your coworker's inboxes at a proper time for them to be able to act on it. Whether they are several time zones away or you are handling email on nights and weekends, the ability to choose when those emails are actually sent can help you look more professional.

Use an Email Strategy Card

Our next solution draws inspiration from the music industry, where recording artist Brian Eno has created a legendary deck of strategy cards for overcoming creative blocks. His cards are called Oblique Strategies, and each one contains a phrase designed to stimulate a different approach to a situation. The cards were designed for music composition and are rather nontraditional in their approach. Examples of these free-thinking phrases for recording artists include "Repetition is a form of change," "Ghost echoes," and "Work at a different speed."

These cards have become almost mythical in the recording industry and have been used by countless music groups, including David Bowie, Coldplay, Phoenix, MGMT, and REM. That's a wonderful resource for recording music, but wouldn't it be nice if we had a different deck of cards for handling difficult professional situations?

With this idea in mind, I created a deck of sixty-four email responses that I use in challenging situations. Volume one of these Email Strategy Cards addresses a wide variety of common situations where we often struggle to find the perfect response.

For example, I have often said yes to requests simply because I didn't have the right words to say no. Can you relate? To help in this situation, the deck includes sixteen different ways to say no without feeling guilty. Saying no more often is a key to success. You might feel a temptation to say that you're busy now, but you could meet next month. The problem is that when next month arrives, you're just as busy and you wish you had declined that meeting in the first place. Saying no more often can free up your calendar. By saying no to low-value requests, we're able to say yes to high-value opportunities when they come our way. Flipping through these cards, I almost always find the perfect phrase to type when I need to tactfully say no.

The deck has other cards as well. There are cards for saying yes while balancing your time wisely, cards for bouncing the ball back into the other person's inbox, and cards for defusing emotionally-charged situations. I created these Email Strategy Cards because I found flipping through an assortment of ready-made phrases makes it easier to find the right words to say—which helps me achieve my goal of spending less time on email. You can obtain these cards by visiting inboxzerosolutions.com.

Keyboard Shortcuts

Using a mouse to navigate your work screen, for the most part, only slows you down. In one moment, your fingers are merrily tapping out a message at a swift pace on the keyboard, then *bzzzzt*. Your brain directs one hand to move from the keyboard to the mouse (or trackpad), to wiggle the wrist until the tiny pointer hovers over the button you're looking for, and then finally to click. Perhaps you push the mouse back to a neutral position, before bringing your hand back to the home row on your keyboard. I'm exaggerating a bit with my description, but try it: see if it doesn't take you two or three seconds to take your hands off the keyboard, click Compose in Gmail (or New Email in Outlook), and then move your hands back to where they started. Let's calculate how much time we're losing to this. If it takes you two seconds for each click—on an email, on the Reply button, on the Send button, and on your inbox—that's eight seconds. Multiply that by 121 email messages per day, and that's sixteen minutes per day, or sixty-seven hours spent every year, merely on mouse clicks.

By using keyboard shortcuts, I found that I could do each of those tasks in less than a quarter second. Not moving my hands from the keyboard is saving me fifty hours every year. You probably already know the shortcuts for copying and pasting text. It's worth learning a few other shortcuts in your email client as well. In Gmail, you first have to enable keyboard shortcuts in the Settings menu (click the gear icon, then click Settings).

There are many shortcuts, but by mastering a few important ones, you'll be able to process your emails significantly faster. Here are the Gmail shortcuts I find most useful:

- In your inbox, press the up and down arrows (or like me, the J and K keys, which don't require you to move your hands from the home position) to navigate through your list of emails. Hit Enter to open the one you want to read.
- To compose an email, press C.
- Reply to an email by pressing R.
- To send an email once you've composed it, press Control+Enter on a PC or Command+Enter on a Mac.
- Return to your inbox from any screen by pressing G (for "go") then I (for "inbox").
- Archive an email by pressing Y.

You can see a full list of Gmail's keyboard shortcuts by pressing the ? key. Outlook and other email clients also have keyboard shortcuts, which you can find easily by searching online.

Action-Oriented Subject Lines

An unfortunate email habit that is likely a holdover from high school essay writing is the pervasive tendency to put the conclusion at the end. We offer background information, rationale, and then finally what we need. The person we're writing to may never make it that far or may stop paying attention.

If you want someone to take action, don't bury your request at the bottom of the email. Put it in the subject. Do you need some data for your upcoming sales presentation? Instead of an amorphous subject like "Sales Presentation," use one that clearly communicates the required action: "I need Q1 sales figures before this Friday." Use the subject line the way a journalist uses a headline—to grab the reader's attention and make a call to action. With close colleagues, I often communicate my entire message in the subject line. For example, "Lunch Thursday? 12:30pm at Bibibop?"

If you don't have a call to action, be considerate and cue the level of importance in your subject line. For example, if you are sharing a new policy, your subject might read: "Just FYI - New Parking Rates." Your coworkers can then decide whether they want to read it or immediately archive it.

Undo Send

One of my favorite features in Gmail is one that gives you up to 30 seconds to "undo" a message you didn't mean to send. This has helped me avoid countless embarrassments after accidentally sending unfinished emails. Search online for "Gmail enable undo send" to find up-to-date instructions for enabling this feature.

Outlook has a similar feature called "Recall this message," but it works only in limited circumstances. The recipient must use Outlook, be in your same organization, and be on the same Microsoft Exchange Server.

Message Templates

If you find yourself repeatedly answering the same question, use an email template to avoid having to type out the same reply again and again. In Gmail it's called Canned Responses, while in Outlook it appears as Quick Parts.

Create standard messages to send driving and parking information, to thank people for sharing requests for new product features, to explain how visitors can reserve a tour online, or to answer whatever questions you seem to receive in the thousands every year.

Recurring Tasks

There are a variety of tasks I take care of on a recurring basis. Every week I approve timesheets, every year I conduct annual reviews, and so on. Trello's free builtin Card Repeater feature automates the process of creating a new card in my Action Items list. Every Wednesday, it creates a card for approving timesheets, and once a year, it adds new cards telling me to prepare the annual review for each of my staff members.

The card appears only when the task needs to be done, so I don't worry about it when it's not relevant, and my list of action items stays truly actionable. I prefer this instead of a calendar reminder, which can come and go on my screen, meaning I might miss it, while a Trello card sticks around and forces me to deal with the task.

Once you've enabled this feature (find instructions by searching online for "enable Trello card repeater"), create template cards for your recurring tasks. First, create a regular card that says, for example, "Approve Timesheets," and on the back of the card, click Repeat under Power-Ups, and set it to create a copy of this card in your Action Items list every week on Wednesday (or whenever you want). That's it. This is the template that will be copied to your Action Items list each week. Now you need a place to store these template cards. I save them to a separate list called "Automations," which I keep at the far right of my Trello board, out of sight and out of mind. The tasks automatically appear at the scheduled intervals in my Action Items list.

I hope you find these Expert Mode suggestions useful and effective. If you have any favorites of your own that you'd like to share, please consider sharing them with me through the book's web site, www.inboxzerosolutions.com

Notes & Sources

Preface

1. **David Allen:** Allen is the creator of Getting Things Done, the immensely popular organizational and productivity system. His best-selling *Getting Things Done: The Art of Stress-Free Productivity* was first published in 2001 (Penguin Books). Citations are from the 2015 revised edition.
2. **Inbox zero:** This term was popularized by productivity expert Merlin Mann, founder of the now-defunct blog *43folders.com*. His Google Tech Talk on inbox zero is available here: https://youtu.be/z9UjeTMb3Yk. David Allen doesn't use this exact term but does write about getting your inbox to "zero" or "empty."

Introduction

1. **Gregory Ciotti quote, "Reading is the supreme lifehack …":** "50 Must-Read Psychology Books," *Sparring Mind* (blog), https://www.sparringmind.com/psychology-books/#more-1140.
2. **Email's humble origins:** The very first version of what would become known as email was invented in 1965 at Massachusetts Institute of Technology (MIT) as part of the university's Compatible Time-Sharing System, which allowed users to share files and messages on a central disk, logging in from remote terminals. Tom Van Vleck, "Electronic Mail and Text Messaging in CTSS, 1965–1973," *IEEE Annals of the History of Computing* 34, no. 1 (January–March 2012): 4–6, doi: 10.1109/MAHC.2012.6.
3. **Text-only messages:** To this day, email is a text-only system. Images and file attachments must be converted to plain text by your email client using a special protocol. This protocol is called MIME, or multipurpose internet mail extensions.
4. **Email overload reported by 85 percent:** This is based on Linda Duxbury's unpublished study on email's impact, "Research Study into Impact of Email on Employees: It's Urgent but is it Important? A Case Study on the Use of Email."

Over 55% of the employees in the study sample reported high levels of email overload and 30% reported moderate levels of email overload.

5. **Gloria Mark's study:** Gloria Mark et al., "Email Duration, Batching and Self-Interruption: Patterns of Email Use on Productivity and Stress," in *Proceedings of ACM CHI 2016* (New York: ACM Press, 2016), 1717–1728. Most of Mark's publications are available on her website: https://www.ics.uci.edu/~gmark/Home_page/Publications.html.

6. **Stanford University study:** Stephen R. Barley, Debra E. Meyerson, and Stine Grodal, "E-mail as a Source and Symbol of Stress," *Organization Science* 22, no. 4 (July–August 2011): 887–906.

7. **Kostadin Kushlev and Elizabeth Dunn's study:** "Checking Email Less Frequently Reduces Stress," *Computers in Human Behavior* 43 (February 2015): 220–228, doi: 10.1016/j.chb.2014.11.005. See also the Future Work Centre's 2015 report *You've Got Mail!*, http://www.futureworkcentre.com/wp-content/uploads/2015/07/FWC-Youve-got-mail-research-report.pdf.

8. **Fire hose:** The term is used in the technology world in various ways to mean "more information than you could possibly want." For example, Twitter has an API called the Firehose, which grants developers access to 500 million tweets per day. The metaphor is a reference to *UHF*, the 1989 film by Weird Al Yankovic, in which a child's prize for winning a game is drinking from a fire hose.

9. **Information overload:** Alvin Toffler discussed this in *Future Shock* (New York: Random House, 1970). The term was mentioned earlier in a 1964 book by Bertram Gross called *The Managing of Organizations* (New York: Free Press of Glencoe), but this book never gained popularity. The book sales tracking service NovelRank lists it #13,791,227 of all time, while *Future Shock* sold over 6 million copies and ranks #48,256.

10. **Adrien Baillet and Johannes Gutenberg:** Ann Blair, *Too Much To Know: Managing Scholarly Information before the Modern Age* (New Haven: Yale University Press, 2010). Around the middle of Blair's information-dense, 416-page book, I couldn't help but realize I was reading a book summarizing the history of book summaries. Adrien Baillet is discussed in Ann Blair, "Reading Strategies for Coping with Information Overload," *Journal of the History of Ideas* 64, no. 1 (January 2003): 11. For an idea of how few books were created each year before the invention of the printing press, see Eltjo Buringh and Jan Luiten Van Zanden's 2009 article "Charting the 'Rise of the West': Manuscripts and Printed Books in Europe, A Long-Term Perspective from the Sixth through Eighteenth Centuries," *The Journal of Economic History* 69, no. 2 (June 2009): Table 3.

11. **Indexes and encyclopedias:** The method of physically cutting and pasting texts to edit and assemble manuscripts was used by Conrad Gesner, Girolamo Cardano, and others (Blair, "Reading Strategies for Coping with Information

Overload," 25–28). Girolamo Cardano appeared to make no secrets of his cutting and pasting. Of all the paintings I have seen of scribes writing books, he is the only one depicted with a pair of scissors prominently displayed among his writing implements. See the cover of Girolamo Cardano, *Mis Libros* (Ediciones Akal, 2002), which can be seen here: https://images-na.ssl-images-amazon.com/images/I/91-oCF3d1zL.jpg.

12. **The average US worker spends 5.2 hours a day on email:** This statistic comes from Adobe's 2017 annual consumer email survey (www.slideshare.net/adobe/adobe-consumer-email-survey-report-2017). Gloria Mark et al. reported 1 hour 23 minutes in "Email Duration, Batching and Self-Interruption."

13. **We're doing emails at night, etc.:** Our tendency to check email at all hours of the day and when we're away from work (at night, before we get out of bed in the morning, during vacation) comes from numerous studies. The Adobe 2017 email study found that 54 percent of those surveyed check email while still in bed in the morning (see slide 13). An IDC/Facebook 2013 study found 80 percent of people check their smartphones within 15 minutes of waking up, and 80 percent of those (so, 64 percent of total respondents) say it's the first thing they do each morning. The report is available on *Adweek* (http://www.adweek.com/digital/smartphones/?red=at). GFI Software's 2015 survey found 2.9 percent checked email while at a funeral. Results were reported as an infographic (https://techtalk.gfi.com/wp-content/uploads/2015/06/DMG-GFI-USreportV4.jpg); the raw data are also available (https://techtalk.gfi.com/hail-mail-or-fail-mail).

Step 1: Pause Your Inbox

1. **Research on email and stress:** The 2017 annual email statistics report by the Radicati Group, a Silicon Valley market research firm, shows the average office worker deals with 121 emails a day. I confirmed with researcher Sara Radicati by phone that this datum was obtained through self-reported surveys. Linda Duxbury of Carleton University in her unpublished "Research Study into Impact of Email on Employees" found a similar number. In a 2017 survey of 1,500 professionals in six organizations, the average participant reported sending and receiving 86 work-related emails at work and 25 at home, for a total of 111 emails a day. Over half reported high levels of work overload and stress, much of it linked to spending more than 30 percent of their time reading and answering emails. Gloria Mark et al. also reported on the connection between email and stress in "The Cost of Interrupted Work: More Speed and Stress," in *Proceedings of the SIGCHI Conference on Human Factors in Computing Systems* (New York: ACM Press, 2008), 107–110.

2. **Stress and its physiological effects:** For a meta-analysis and review of literature on heart-rate variability, see Hye-Geum Kim et al., "Stress and Heart Rate

Variability: A Meta-Analysis and Review of the Literature," *Psychiatry Investigation* 15, no. 3 (March 2018): 235–245, doi: 10.30773/pi.2017.08.17.

3. **Stress, headaches, and heart rate variability:** One of many studies on the topic is Muhammad Abid Azam et al., "Individuals with Tension and Migraine Headaches Exhibit Increased Heart Rate Variability during Post-Stress Mindfulness Meditation Practice but a Decrease during a Post-Stress Control Condition: A Randomized, Controlled Experiment," *International Journal of Psychophysiology* 110 (December 2016): 66–74, doi: 10.1016/j.ijpsycho.2016.10.011.

4. **Stress and cortisol production:** For a study on stress-induced cortisol production's interference with learning and memory, see Susanne Vogel and Lars Schwabe, "Learning and Memory under Stress: Implications for the Classroom," *npj Science of Learning* 1 (2016), article no. 16011, https://www.nature.com/articles/npjscilearn201611. Regarding cortisol's effects on the immune system, see William McK. Jefferies, "Cortisol and Immunity," *Medical Hypotheses* 34, no. 3 (March 1991): 198–208.

5. **Precommitment and Odysseus:** Roy F. Baumeister and John Tierney, *Willpower* (New York: The Penguin Press, 2011), 151.

6. **We have a fixed amount of willpower each day:** The concept of a fixed amount of daily willpower comes from research by Roy Baumeister, described in his best-selling book *Willpower*. For a synopsis, see the excellent article in *The Atlantic*: Hans Villarica, "The Chocolate-and-Radish Experiment That Birthed the Modern Conception of Willpower," *The Atlantic*, April 12, 2012, https://www.theatlantic.com/health/archive/2012/04/the-chocolate-and-radish-experiment-that-birthed-the-modern-conception-of-willpower/255544/. The many studies that support this idea include Marina Milyavskaya and Michael Inzlicht, "What's So Great about Self-Control?" *Social Psychological and Personality Science* 8, no 6 (2017): 603–611, doi: 10.1177/1948550616679237; Veronika Job, Carol S. Dweck, and Gregory M. Walton, "Ego Depletion—Is It All in Your Head?" *Psychological Science* 21, no. 11 (2010): 1686–1693, doi: 10.1177/0956797610384745; Mark Muraven and Roy F. Baumeister, "Self-Regulation and Depletion of Limited Resources: Does Self-Control Resemble a Muscle?" *Psychological Bulletin* 126, no. 2 (2000): 247–259; and Roy Baumeister, Ellen Bratslavsky, Mark Muraven, and Dianne M. Tice, "Ego Depletion: Is the Active Self a Limited Resource?" *Journal of Personality and Social Psychology* 74, no. 5 (1998): 1252–1265.

7. **Cellphone pouches:** These are used in high schools as well as universities (e.g., Boston University). Performing artists such as Chris Rock and Ariana Grande have also required their use at concerts. See Tovia Smith, "A School's Way to Fight Phones in Class: Lock 'Em Up," *NPR* online, January 11, 2018, https://www.npr.org/2018/01/11/577101803/a-schools-way-to-fight-phones-in-class-lock-em-up.

8. **We check email 74 times per day:** Gloria Mark et al., "Focused, Aroused, but So Distractible," *Proceedings of the 18th ACM Conference on Computer Supported*

Cooperative Work & Social Computing (New York: ACM, 2015), 903–916. Wanting to avoid hyperbole, I used a conservative figure. Other studies have cited higher figures. Karen Renaud, Judith Ramsey, and Mario Hair's 2006 study reported 36 times per hour, or 288 checks per day ("'You've Got E-Mail!' . . . Shall I Deal With It Now? Electronic Mail From the Recipient's Perspective," *International Journal of Human–Computer Interaction* 21, no. 3 (2006): 313–332).

9.   **We check smartphones 76 times per day:** The figures cited here are from dscout's 2016 study *Mobile Touches* (https://blog.dscout.com/hubfs/downloads/dscout _mobile_touches_study_2016.pdf): Android users check 76 times per day, iPhone owners unlock 80 times per day, and Nokia users check 144 times per day. Since a lot of items are now available on the lock screen, these figures include phone checking regardless of whether users unlocked the phone. The figures from dscout are relatively conservative; other studies claim that we check our phones even more frequently.

10.   **Cognitive slot machine:** This term is used by Tom Stafford, professor of psychology at the University of Sheffield. See Drake Baer, "The Internet is Like A Slot Machine," *Fast Company*, May 29, 2013, https://www.fastcompany .com/3010168/how-the-internet-is-like-a-slot-machine-and-why-its-easy- to-get-lost-in-it; Suw Charman-Anderson, "Breaking the Email Compulsion," *The Guardian*, August 27, 2008, https://www.theguardian.com/technology/ 2008/aug/28/email.addiction.

11.   **Task switching and context switching:** Gerald Weinberg was the first person to apply the term *context switching* to humans, in his book *Quality Software Management*. Before then psychologists used the term *task switching* in their research. For example: Robert Rogers and Stephpen Monsell, "The Costs of a Predictable Switch between Simple Cognitive Tasks," *Journal of Experimental Psychology: General* 124 (1995): 207–231, doi: 10.1037/0096- 3445.124.2.207. The reference list for Rogers and Monsell's article contains multiple examples of task-switching studies.

12.   **Time lost to context switching:** Thomas Jackson, Ray Dawson, and Darren Wilson claim 64 seconds in their study of an IT company, "Case Study: Evaluating the Effect of Email Interruptions within the Workplace" (presentation, Conference on Empirical Assessment in Software Engineering EASE 2002, Keele, UK, April 2002), https://dspace.lboro.ac.uk/2134/489. Mark et al. report 23 minutes and 15 seconds in "The Cost of Interrupted Work."

13.   **Context switching simulation:** The exercise is based on the Multitasking Name Game created by Swedish software coach Henrik Kniberg. The original game and Kniberg's article about it can be found here: https://www.crisp.se/gratis -material-och-guider/multitasking-name-game.

14.   **Ford assembly line:** Ford himself was more a sponsor than the inventor of the assembly line, which was designed by his talented team, according to Charles

E. Sorensen's 1956 memoir *My Forty Years with Ford* (Detroit, MI: Wayne State University; see p. 116).

15. **Starbucks drink times:** "At Starbucks, Every Second Counts," *Chicago Tribune*, April 13, 2005, http://articles.chicagotribune.com/2005-04-13/news/0504130351_1_chain-of-coffee-shops-starbucks-blended.

16. **Batching emails:** A greater feeling of productivity was seen with email batching behaviors in Mark et al.'s 2016 study, "Email Duration, Batching and Self-interruption." This is also reported by Kushlev and Dunn, "Checking Email Less Frequently Reduces Stress."

17. **Phoning while driving increases your errors by over 100 percent:** David L. Strayer and William A. Johnston, "Driven to Distraction: Dual-Task Studies of Simulated Driving and Conversing on a Cellular Telephone," *Psychological Science* 12, no. 6 (2000): 462–466, doi: 10.1111/1467-9280.00386.

18. **College professors and confidence bias:** K. Patricia Cross, "Not Can, But *Will* College Teaching Be Improved?" *New Directions for Higher Education* 17 (1977): 1–15, doi: 10.1002/he.36919771703.

19. **Drivers and confidence bias:** Ola Svenson, "Are We All Less Risky and More Skillful than Our Fellow Drivers?" *Acta Psychologica* 47 (1981): 143–148.

20. **Multitasking:** The research in this area is prolific. Here are a few good sources to get you started. Christine Rosen published a wonderful overview of multitasking research in *The New Atlantis* ("The Myth of Multitasking," Spring 2008, https://www.thenewatlantis.com/publications/the-myth-of-multitasking). Clifford Nass's 2009 study on multitasking is Eyal Ophir, Clifford Nass, and Anthony D. Wagner, "Cognitive Control in Media Multitaskers," *Proceedings of the National Academy of Sciences* 106, no, 37 (September 2009): 15583–15587, http://www.pnas.org/content/106/37/15583.full. Search for his talks on YouTube; he is a very engaging speaker. See also David Sanbonmatsu et al., "Who Multi-Tasks and Why? Multi-Tasking Ability, Perceived Multi-Tasking Ability, Impulsivity, and Sensation Seeking," *PLoS ONE* 8, no. 1: e54402, doi: 10.1371/journal.pone.0054402.

21. **Charles Peachock:** Telephone interview conducted on October 23, 2017.

22. **UK study of 2,000 professionals:** Future Work Centre, *You've Got Mail!*

23. **Graphic of email checking patterns:** Adapted from Jack Reeves, "How I 'Batch Process' Email Only 2–3 Times a Day," *PRSUIT*, https://prsuit.com/life-in-review/how-i-batch-process-email-only-2-3-times-a-day/.

24. **Batching email and stress:** This is a nascent field, and there are some inconsistencies in how people measure this. For example, Mark et al. in "Email Duration, Batching and Self-interruption" found that batching does not reduce stress; however, her idea of batching is different than mine. Her batchers are no less stressed on average than non-batchers; however, the batchers in her study batch either because they have to (due to large blocks of meetings) or

just happen to (not because of a particular strategy). In either case, they are no more likely to have finished their email and their inboxes remain full of messages.

Step 2: Get to Zero

1. **Interviews on email habits:** From 2017 to 2018, I conducted over 100 informal in-person and phone interviews with professionals from various fields. Participants included university professors, radio and podcast producers, event organizers, human resources professionals, and university vice presidents. "Give up the fantasy" is from one of these interviews.

2. **Checkers and finishers:** This lingo was inspired by Barry Schwartz's discussion of "pickers" and "choosers" in his book *The Paradox of Choice: Why More Is Less* (New York: HarperCollins, 2004). Schwartz, in turn, may have found his inspiration from Nobel Prize–winning economist Herbert A. Simon's categorization of "maximizers" and "satisficers" in "Rational Choice and the Structure of the Environment," *Psychological Review* 63, no. 2 (March 1956): 129–138, doi: 10.1037/h0042769.

3. **Alex Iskold:** He has written about his use of inbox zero on his blog: https://alexiskold.net/2014/03/17/inbox-0/.

4. **Joe Robinson quote, "Vagueness is the enemy ...":** Robinson is a motivational speaker who coaches professionals on achieving better work-life balance. The original quote came from his article "The Science of Why We Burn Out and Don't Have To," https://www.worktolive.info/blog/the-science-of-why-we-burn-out-and-dont-have-to.

5. **Jessica Kerr quote, "Pretend your brain...":** This is from her Twitter feed: https://twitter.com/jessitron/status/369496945879810050. Her website is jessitron.com.

6. **Medieval quarry worker's creed:** Quoted in Andy Hunt and Dave Thomas, *The Pragmatic Programmer: From Journeyman to Master* (Reading, MA: Addison-Wesley Longman, 2000), xx.

7. **4D technique:** This was developed by Sally McGhee and David Allen when they were business partners, and each share intellectual property on this material. Both went on to write successful books on self-organization. Sally McGhee and John Wittry, *Take Back Your Life!* (Microsoft Press, 2007); Allen, "Processing: Getting 'In' to Empty," chapter 6 in *Getting Things Done*.

8. **Approximately half of our email is not actionable:** This applies to my personal inbox but also more authoritatively from Victoria Bellotti et al.'s study "Quality Versus Quantity: E-Mail-Centric Task Management and Its Relation with Overload," *Human-Computer Interaction* 20, no. 1 (2005): 89–138. Figure 2 in that study presents the types of activities in the emails received by study

participants: "Announcements" (35 percent) and "Not an Activity" (8 percent) are both nonactionable; I also reasoned that "Dialogue, Discussion, Negotiation" inarguably included emails on which the recipient was copied and did not require action by the recipient.

9. **Forty-two hours a year organizing email:** I presumed a typical five-day work week with two weeks vacation, which means 250 workdays a year. I also rounded the resulting 41.67 hours to the nearest hour.

10. **Sheena Iyengar and Mark Lepper's jam experiment:** Sheena S. Iyengar and Mark R. Lepper, "When Choice is Demotivating: Can One Desire Too Much of a Good Thing?" *Journal of Personality and Social Psychology* 79, no. 6 (2000): 995–1006, doi: 10.1037//0022-3514.79.6.995.

11. **Proctor & Gamble and Golden Cat sales data:** Sheena Iyengar and Kanika Agrawal, "A Better Choosing Experience," *strategy+business* 61, November 23, 2010, https://www.strategy-business.com/article/00046.

12. **Steve Jobs and Apple's product mix:** The changes Jobs made to the product lineup when he returned to Apple are well known and have been widely reported. One source is Walter Isaacon's "The Real Leadership Lessons of Steve Jobs," *Harvard Business Review* (April 2012), https://hbr.org/2012/04/the-real-leadership-lessons-of-steve-jobs. Data on Apple's computer sales can be found on *Statista* (https://www.statista.com/statistics/263444/sales-of-apple-mac-computers-since-first-quarter-2006/).

13. **Maximizers and satisficers:** *Satisficer* is a portmanteau of *satisfying* and *sufficing*. Simon developed the idea in a 1956 paper as a way of explaining a particular form of decision making, or cognitive heuristic. See Simon, "Rational Choice and the Structure of the Environment."

14. **Drew Carey:** Susan Young, "How Personal Development Saved Drew Carey's Life," *Success* (December 3, 2015), https://www.success.com/article/how-personal-development-saved-drew-careys-life; Tierney and Baumeister, *Willpower*, 75–76, 84–86.

15. **Open loops:** This concept is from David Allen's *Getting Things Done*, specifically from step 1 (Collect) of his 5-step process. Collecting open loops means to scan your mind (and office and house) and record every unfinished task.

16. **Zeigarnik effect:** Bluma Zeigarnik, "On Finished and Unfinished Tasks," in *A Source Book of Gestalt Psychology*, edited by Willis Davis Ellis (New York: Humanities Press, 1967), 300–314. The chapter is available online: http://codeblab.com/wp-content/uploads/2009/12/On-Finished-and-Unfinished-Tasks.pdf.

17. **Short-circuit the Zeigarnik effect:** E. J. Masicampo and Roy F. Baumeister, "Consider It Done! Plan Making Can Eliminate the Cognitive Effects of Unfulfilled Goals," *Journal of Personality and Social Psychology* 101, no. 4 (October 2011): 667–683, http://users.wfu.edu/masicaej/MasicampoBaumeister2011JPS.pdf. Neuroscientist Daniel J. Levitin comes to the same conclusion as Masicampo

and Baumeister through a biological rather than a psychological approach. He describes how writing things down can deactivate mental notifications in the "rehearsal" regions of your brain in his book *The Organized Mind: Thinking Straight in the Age of Information Overload* (New York: Dutton, 2014).

18. **David Allen quote, "Most people have never…":** Baumeister and Tierney, *Willpower*, 78.

19. **"Mind like water":** Allen, *Getting Things Done*, 10–11.

Step 3: Leave It Paused

1. **Merlin Mann quote, "It's about how to reclaim…":** This is from a *Lifehack* article by Mike Vardy, "The Ultimate Way to get to Inbox Zero," www.lifehack.org/articles/lifehack/ultimate-way-inbox-zero.html.

2. **One thing:** Gary Keller and Jay Papasan, *One Thing* (Austin, TX: Bard Press, 2013).

3. **Julie Morgenstern:** *Never Check Email in the Morning* (New York: Simon & Schuster, 2004).

4. **Clifford Nass's 2009 study on multitasking:** Ophir, Nass, and Wagner, "Cognitive Control in Media Multitaskers." Nass's comments about the study are from an interview with Ira Flatow on NPR's *Science Friday* ("The Myth of Multitasking," *NPR* online, May 10, 2013, www.npr.org).

5. **Willpower is like a muscle:** Kelly McGonigal, *The Willpower Instinct: How Self-Control Works, Why It Matters, and What You Can Do to Get More of It* (New York: Penguin Group, 2012). McGonigal, a professor of psychology at Stanford, presents a set of science-backed approaches for achieving greater self-control, involving everything from proper sleep and exercise to gamification of self-improvement.

6. **Implementation intentions:** Peter Gollwitzer has published numerous studies on implementation intentions since the late 1990s. The most recent is Maik Bieleke, Eve Legrand, Astrid Mignon, and Peter Gollwitzer, "More than Planned: Implementation Intention Effects in Non-Planned Situations," *Acta Psychologica* 184 (March 2018): 64–74, doi: 10.1016/j.actpsy.2017.06.003. For a meta-analysis of 94 studies on the topic, see Peter Gollwitzer and Paschal Sheeran, "Implementation Intentions and Goal Achievement: A Meta-Analysis of Effects and Processes," *Advances in Experimental Social Psychology* 38 (2006): 69–119, doi: 10.1016/S0065-2601(06)38002-1.

7. **Study with 91 percent success of if-then plans:** Sarah Milne, Sheina Orbell, and Paschal Sheeran, "Combining Motivational and Volitional Interventions to Promote Exercise Participation: Protection Motivation Theory and Implementation Intentions," *British Journal of Health Psychology* 7 (2002): 173.

8. **MIT if-then implementation intention exercise:** Paschal Sheeran, Richard Aubrey, and Stephen Kellett, "Increasing Attendance for Psychotherapy: Implementation Intentions and the Self-Regulation of Attendance-Related Negative Affect," *Journal of Consulting and Clinical Psychology* 75 (2007): 853–863.

9. **Marshmallow study:** Walter Mischel, Ebbe. B. Ebbesen, and Antoinette Raskoff Zeiss, "Cognitive and Attentional Mechanisms in Delay of Gratification," *Journal of Personality and Social Psychology* 21, no. 2 (1972): 204–218, doi: 10.1037/h0032198.

10. **The marshmallow test recreation video on YouTube:** https://www.youtube.com/watch?v=QX_oy9614HQ.

11. **Marshmallow study participants and SAT scores:** Walter Mischel, Yuichi Shoda, Monica L. Rodriguzez, "Delay of Gratification in Children," *Science* 244 (1989): 933–938, doi: 10.1126/science.2658056.

12. **Marshmallow study participants, 40 years later:** B. J. Casey et al., "Behavioral and Neural Correlates of Delay of Gratification 40 Years Later," *Proceedings of the National Academy of Sciences* 108, no. 36 (2011), 14998–15003, doi: 10.1073/pnas.1108561108.

13. **Baumeister's radish and chocolate experiment:** Roy F. Baumeister et al., "Ego Depletion: Is the Active Self a Limited Resource?" *Journal of Personality and Social Psychology* 74, no. 5 (May 1998): 1252–1265.

14. **Chip and Dan Heath quote, "For anything to change …":** *Switch: How to Change Things When Change Is Hard* (New York: Broadway Books, 2010), 4.

15. **We stare longer at negative photographs:** Numerous studies have shown this. One is Susan T. Fiske, "Attention and Weight in Person Perception: The Impact of Negative and Extreme Behavior," *Journal of Personality and Social Psychology* 38 (1980): 389–906.

16. **We are more upset about losing $50:** This has been shown various studies, such as Amos Tversky and Daniel Kahneman, "The Framing of Decisions and the Psychology of Choice," *Science* 211 (1981): 453–458.

17. **Language is more negative than positive:** James Averill found that 62 percent of the 588 emotional words in English are negative; see *A Semantic Atlas of Emotional Concepts* (American Psychological Association, 1975). Chip and Dan Heath also discuss this in *Switch.* The fact that negative emotions predominate across languages was studied by Robert Schrauf, "The Preponderance of Negative Emotion Words in the Emotion Lexicon: A Cross-generational and Cross-linguistic Study" *Journal of Multilingual and Multicultural Development* 25, no. 2–3 (2014): 266–284.

18. **Marriage and positive events:** The "magic ratio" of five positive interactions to one negative interaction was posited by John Gottman and Robert Levenson. See Kyle Benson, "The Magic Ratio, According to Science," *The Gottman Institute Blog,* October 4, 2017, www.gottman.com/blog/the-magic-relationship-ratio-according-science/.

19. **"Bad is stronger than good":** Baumeister et al., "Bad is Stronger than Good," *Review of General Psychology* 5, no. 4 (2001): 323–370, doi: 10.1037//1089-2680.5.4.323.

20. **Steve Wozniak quotes:** Stephen Wozniak, "Homebrew and How the Apple Came to Be," in *Digital Deli: The Comprehensive, User-Lovable Menu of Computer Lore, Culture, Lifestyles and Fancy*, ed. Steve Ditlea (New York: Workman Publishing, 1984).

21. **Motivator and hygiene factors:** Frederick Herzberg, "The Motivation-Hygiene Concept and Problems of Manpower," *Personnel Administration* 27, no. 1, (1964): 3–7; Frederick Herzberg, "One More Time: How Do You Motivate Employees?" *Harvard Business Review* 46, no. 1 (January–February 1968): 53–62.

22. **Study of 12,000 corporate employees:** Teresa Amabile and Steven J. Kramer, "Inner Work Life: Understanding the Subtext of Business Performance," *Harvard Business Review* 85, no. 5 (May 2007): 72–83, https://hbr.org/2007/05/inner-work-life-understanding-the-subtext-of-business-performance.

23. **Books like Deep Work, Flow, and Drive:** A more complete list of books connecting meaningful work to motivation would surely have to include Malcolm Gladwell's *Outliers: The Story of Success* and Dan Ariely's *Payoff: The Hidden Logic That Shapes Our Motivations*.

Expert Mode

1. **Speech averages 150 words per minute:** C. R. Benz, *Effects of Time Compressed Speech upon the Comprehension of a Visual Oriented Television Lecture* (unpublished doctoral dissertation), Wayne State University, 1971. The rate of normal speech ranges from 120 to 180 words per minute according to Alan H. Monroe and Douglas Ehninger, *Principles and Types of Speech Communication* (Glenview, IL: Scott Foresman, 1974).

2. **Average typing speed as 45 words per minute:** This figure is based on two studies. Average typing speed was measured at 58 words per minute by Anna Maria Feit, Daryl Weir, and Antti Oulasvirta, "How We Type: Movement Strategies and Performance in Everyday Typing," *Proceedings of the 2016 CHI Conference on Human Factors in Computing Systems* (New York: ACM 201), 4262–4273. Average typing speed of undergraduates was measured at 33 words per minute by Nina Keith and K. Anders Ericsson, "A Deliberate Practice Account of Typing Proficiency in Everyday Typists," *Journal of Experimental Psychology: Applied* 13, no. 3 (2007): 135.

3. **Reading speed as 280 words per minute:** Tammie Calef, Marcie Pieper, and Bradley Coffey, "Comparisons of Eye Movements Before and After a Speed-Reading Course," *Journal of the American Optometric Association* 70 (1999): 171–181.

4. **Cal Newport quote, "Synchronous conversation…":** Cal Newport, "A Modest Proposal: Eliminate Email," *Harvard Business Review* online, February 18, 2016, https://hbr.org/2016/02/a-modest-proposal-eliminate-email.

5. **Brian Eno's Oblique Strategies cards:** The cards are available on his website: www.enoshp.co.uk. These legendary cards inspired a variety of similar card decks in other fields. For example, the global design company IDEO's Methods Cards is another well-known set, used to spark design thinking (www.ideo.com/post/method-cards). MethodKit, which also produces a series of card decks to inspire creativity in varied contexts, has an encyclopedic listing of 81 creativity card decks on its website (methodkit.com/research-method-cards/).

Made in United States
Orlando, FL
27 June 2023

34568829R00057